HEALING SEXUALITY

A PLEIADIAN PERSPECTIVE

ROB GAUTHIER

THE ET WHISPERER

KALAMAZOO, MI

Healing Sexuality/Rob Gauthier -- 1st ed.

ISBN 9798875954894

If you follow your heart, your heart is connected directly to your Higher Self and Soul. And your Soul knows better than anyone, for you. It knows better than the wisest, or longest living entity in this universe. Because it IS you, it is part of you and it is what you need. So follow the heart and you will never be led wrong.

TReb Bor Yit-NE

CONTENTS

FOREWARD

Greetings everyone. My name is Rob Gauthier and I am a professional channeler. I have been called the ET Whisperer because I have channeled thousands of unique extraterrestrial races through my work. I am so happy you are here and am truly excited to share the material contained in this book and as brought through by my guide Aridif.

This book on Healing Sexuality was channeled by my guide Aridif. I began channeling Aridif more than a decade ago. He was introduced to me by another guide of mine, TReb Bor yit-NE. Treb explained that in a similar way that I communicated with him for guidance and wisdom, Treb did the same with Aridif.

Aridif describes himself as an ancient Pleiadian from the Deneb star system. His race is a Type One race and on the upper end of Sixth Density. That means that they are in the final stage of evolution before leaving the physical incarnation cycle. They have worked with Earth and the Human Collective Consciousness for many thousands of years.

Aridif differentiates between Type One and Type Two beings. Type One beings recognize and honor the connection between all life. They perceive all entities as part of a larger collective that is all part of Source, Creator, All That Is. Type One beings will offer guidance and share information with others, but they will not infringe upon free will. They are committed to non-interference.

Type Two beings exist on a spectrum of benevolence to malevolence. They also will 'get involved' so to speak. Highly benevolent Type Two races do so out of a desire to assist.

Highly malevolent Type Two races intervene often to further their agendas and desires.

As a Type One being, Aridif is committed to non-interference and always respects free will. These are two of the reasons I have come to trust the information and guidance he shares. I also know that he has witnessed the evolution of the Earth Human Collective Consciousness from its inception to the current shift on December 21, 2021, into Fourth Density.

While brainstorming for upcoming courses late in 2022 and deciding on which topics to prioritize, I asked Aridif what information would be most useful and healing to Humanity at its current stage of evolution. An issue that those on Earth struggle with and creates a great deal of resistance in humans. His answer was sexuality.

As Aridif will explain in detail, sexuality has been an issue for humans since the forced jump in evolution between second and third density that Humanity experienced thousands of years ago. According to Aridif, Earth Humans were only two-thirds of the way through their Second Density journey when the Annunaki altered human genetics to forcibly move the species into third density. This was a jump of several thousand years. This created a great deal of resistance in the collective.

According to Aridif, most races that make the transition into fourth density have worked through their issues with sexuality. However, from his perspective, these issues remain unresolved on Earth. He also stated that humanity was ready to receive information that had previously not been shared and to take steps to heal its relationship with sexuality.

Thus was birthed a series of channelings that would become the course on Healing Sexuality and eventually take the form of this book you are now reading.

This book contains Aridif's four direct course channelings. A question and answer section follows each of the four channelings. These questions were submitted by the original course participants so they could receive more clarity on the topics Aridif discussed and support their process of moving through the material.

I hope that you find the information and techniques contained in this book useful on your path to growth and healing. As you heal your issues around sexuality, self-love, and self-acceptance, you offer that energy template and support to all others in the Earth Collective Consciousness who might be dealing with similar lessons.

Finally, as Aridif states at the beginning of every channeling, know that you are loved.

PART ONE · TECHNICAL ASPECTS OF HUMAN SEXUALITY AND ENERGY MECHANICS

Greetings to all this is Aridif. That is A R I D I F. And this is it spelled. We understand that all of you desire to understand more about sexual trauma. How it relates to the human collective, how it is perceived within your own collective consciousness. And how to work with releasing that trauma indeed. But before diving into these topics and queries we will express what in our own perspective is of the utmost importance.

First, we express that you are loved. Above and beyond all things expressed in this day, to know, feel, and to perceive this love is of the greatest importance. Secondly, it is our greatest excitement, and within that same great excitement in which we co-create with you, not only in this moment but in all moments of your perceived time linearly. And, of course, we will now dive into the topic at hand.

First, as you are looking through the construct technical attributes of human sexuality, the energetic mechanics of co-creation, creation, individual understanding, part of the energy fields, the Human Collective Consciousness as a singular entity into your collective consciousness. Sexuality affects all beings within the earth. Yes, all beings, whether you are pansexual, whether you are heterosexual, homosexual, bisexual, or asexual - all of these are interpreted around sexuality.

But first, what is sexuality in the physical essence? The physical essence of sexuality combines something that you already understand and know anatomically. Something that you already understand genetically. Something that you already understand with the physical body in the act of co-creating and creating sexuality, the act of touching your sexuality with your energy and the constructs beyond. But we will share first the physical attributes alone, as these are very important.

First of all, sexuality is physical attributes that are dictated by your physical structure, your mental body, your related energy that is within your second chakra, and physically that energy manifests through the hormones that your body produces.

First of all, sexuality is physical attributes that are dictated by your physical structure, your mental body, your related energy that is within your second chakra, and physically that energy manifests through the hormones that your body produces. Of course, the masculine forms holding testosterone to be the more dominant chemicals that are released anatomically and of course, estrogen being that which is created from that feminine archetype body. And, of course, both groups of humans hold both of the attributes of these chemicals.

Yet passageway of those chemicals through your body, the amount of these chemicals through your body, dictates greatly whether you hold a more masculine form or feminine form, even as all of you have understood that an entity who was born biologically as a masculine or male being can create an experience of holding hormones within their body that are estrogen-related and hold more feminine energy. Just as those who are born into female or feminine bodies take that which is testosterone and become more masculine, embodying the masculine energy much more deeply. So, of course, there are physical attributes to this construct.

Genetically, we must go back to the ancestry of your human perspective and race.

Genetically, we must go back to the ancestry of your human perspective and race. Humans in the first iteration were, of course, entities that your own history does not yet fully understand. There is the missing link that is involved with human evolution.

But, of course, what comes before and what comes after is not through your normal means of evolution. From your bodies, of course, from your own genetics. This construct was a co-creation upon extraterrestrial entities that would intervene and interfere with the natural flow of human evolution.

These entities brought about their own DNA and gave their DNA to human consciousness, and, of course, creating the new human. And, of course, after this, there were several iterations in turn that created the human that you understand and know in this day. From over 2,250,000 years previous to the Annunaki's first manipulation of your DNA, all of the way to several tens of thousands of years ago, approximately at 23,000 years.

The last DNA manipulation was given and there were seven changes that occurred utilizing the DNA of twelve races. And, of course, you have heard seven and twelve being that of holding sacred numbers. This is due to the nature of your change as a human being.

So what was the first human being? You understand by looking at the ancestors that you did understand and did know before the 2,250,000 to 2,750,000 year mark, and these entities were more so as monkey-formed consciousness by many human standards, although in our own perspective, it is much less as a monkey as you would understand and know it in this day, and fully evolved consciousness that were human beings at that time.

Comparative to this moment is more so as your Bigfoot entities. The beings that you know as Sasquatch or Bigfoot. And in that term. These were what humans could have been unfettered, could have been undisturbed, and could have been unrelented in the processing of other consciousnesses in the co-creation and a form of that creation.

Humans in that way would have created a sexuality much different than what you have in this time.

So what occurs at this point changes not just your physical body, but genetics and DNA as well. The chemical processes in which it works also changes. You have your glandular system that is responsible for the productive units in your physical body. They do not work the same as they would had they not been interacted with or interrupted in that time. Humans in that way would have created a sexuality much different than what you have in this time.

Part of this is the guilt that comes from many of the races that co-created with human beings. Even those that were the Annunaki, who saw you as pets, who saw you as working-class animals, still interacted sexually with human beings to create offspring.

Now we understand those who know the physical structure of the human body and its relations create the form of the Rh positive and Rh negative blood styles. And the only reason that there is no uniformity there is that all of the entities who hold genetics predisposed to that of the negative blood systems are energetically linked to the ancestors that they held, which sexually interacted with those of the Annunaki.

Of course, those who hold the positive blood type may still hold ancestors who had sexual interactions. But the way the energy comes to the surface of the physicality in those that are Rh negative, of course, is directly related to those entities.

Now you find that of the human collective had genetic changes. Changes that were laboratory-formed and scientific in nature, much as that which you see your own scientists do when cloning animals or cloning ears on mice, but done so at a higher level of understanding. And even though there are many races who hold even higher levels of understanding than that of the Annunaki, still hold the energy of the Annunaki in order to make such changes.

Now, with the Annunaki changes that came,
the guilt that came from several races such as
the Annunaki, such as the Elohim, such as the

Pleiadian, Sirian, Arcturian, and Reptilian beings that exist within your lineage and bloodline, all held some level of resistance as it pertains to humans.

Now, with the Annunaki changes that came, the guilt that came from several races such as the Annunaki, such as the Elohim, such as the Pleiadian, Sirian, Arcturian, and Reptilian beings that exist within your lineage and bloodline, all held some level of resistance as it pertains to humans. Some of them felt guilty. Some of them were angry at the changes that either were done to humans before their intervention or after. Some of them saw you as property, creating an imbalance, not seeing the equality and oneness within you, and yet others simply perceived it to be a bad idea.

Now, of course, some of these races interacted with humans in a sexual fashion, although the only reproductive form of sexual exchange that came from the current timeline of human beings were that of the Annunaki.

Now, of course, some of these races interacted with humans in a sexual fashion, although the only reproductive form of sexual exchange that came from the current timeline of human beings were that of the Annunaki. Even though Earth-based reptilians have had sexual interactions with human beings, although the entities that were Pleiadian and Sirian had sexual interactions with human beings, of course, these entities did not bear children, and so their children did not hold large lineages.

Part of this has to do with a cleansing of human beings. You hear about this through your own understanding of the Bible and the great flood. The Egyptian forms of the great floods, the Greek stories of the great floods, the Roman stories of the great floods, the Incan, Mayan, all of Indian cultures within, understood one form of destruction from the greater earth itself. This, of course, came from the cleanse of all bloodlines that were not expressed as acceptable for the Annunaki's iteration.

Of course, the Annunaki revisited Human Collective Consciousness a second time after manipulation had already taken place after their initial manipulation. This was more so to teach humans. There was a greater understanding after several generations. An understanding known as we did the wrong thing with these humans. We must leave them in a better place in which they were.

The first iteration brought great psychic abilities to human beings. Brought a great expression of expanded forms of consciousness to human beings. And with that expanded form of consciousness for the human being, these entities left the human beings to fend for themselves. Left the human beings to be manipulated with a lesser form of psychic understanding and less a form of mental attributes that could progress forth.

Of course, there will be great imbalance in an entire collective when that collective is created from many different broken experiences and many different broken parts of energies that were involved in creation and co-creation.

And now the physicality of all of these races, the energy behind the genetics and the physicality before, come down into the body. This gives you the feel of sexuality for the human race. Of course, there will be great imbalance in an entire collective when that collective is created from many different broken experiences and many different broken parts of energies that were involved in creation and co-creation.

Now as we express the term broken we do not see you as broken. We understand you see yourself as broken in many ways as a greater collective. You see the walls that you have with one another, the greed that comes with one another, the murders that occur with one another. But most of all, humans perceive sexuality at one of the higher rates of understanding. You are charged with a great sexual, animalistic drive of that of your reptilian counterparts who hold the genetics that they have shared with you.

Part of this was due to the Annunaki, who also held fifty percent of their own lineage from feminine Pleiadian beings. And in an attempt to masculinize themselves, they created a form of connection with ancient reptilian blood and did so without permission. So, of course, it brought the attention of that of ancient reptilians and also brought attention from all of the other beings in which co-created with humans afterward.

Now come down into your body away from your history and back into your Now Moment. See yourself in this moment. See the physical attributes of your own sexuality. Of course, the majority of humans hold in one of two categories either the masculine physical form or feminine physical form. The masculine that is born with the construct of masculine energy flowing through, and in one form or another either develops a penis or was born without a penis as well. And of course, the feminine energy flowing through the body, understanding the reproductive system, holding a vagina at birth or a vagina that is given at a later time.

Now we understand transgenderism is a part of the human experience which holds some forms of contention. And, of course, we will speak in depth about this as we go forward. But it must be recognized whether it is perceived as a positive or negative construct for the individual who hears this.

All of these forms in the physical structure are felt. And as most energies and organs are part of a greater system, with the exception of the spine and the exception of the brain, are localized to one region only.

There's a part of that energy that plays a great role in human sexuality in general, has a great part of heterosexuality in the human collective in general, homosexuality in general, in your human collective. All of these forms in the physical structure are felt. And as most energies and organs are part of a greater system, with the exception of the spine and the exception of the brain, are localized to one region only. Yet the penis and vagina are connected to nearly all portions of the human physical structure.

Think of yourself as you are going through the act of sexuality, be it by yourself or with other human consciousnesses. In that way, your sexuality being aroused creates sensations throughout the entirety of your body and creates a heightened sense of mental and emotional essences brought forward and to the surface in positive and negative ways expressed.

And of course, the energy can go from a slight sensation of stimulation throughout the body or as deeply as the bottom of your feet, tingling severely to the top of your head, feeling light. All things that are within that structure of your physical body, the mental forms, the emotional forms, energetic forms are all existing and tied to what is occurring with your penis or vagina.

Now as you understand the nature of yourself.
You can start to understand the nature of others.

Now as you understand the nature of yourself. You can start to understand the nature of others. When you perceive yourself as a masculine being, holding that of a penis and stimulation with that penis, you can understand the nature of other human beings who also have penises.

Now of course, there are humans within both human and masculine bodies that have a form of skin removal at birth, mutilation to the genitalia of that entity. And this is done in many cultures to either or both sexes.

Now as this occurs, even if it is that of a spiritual practice or religious ideology. This does take energy away from that construct. It takes not only sensitivity of sexual co-creation but also the energy of your second chakra connection and all of the energies that are involved in this first step of your physicality at the very first portion of your life on Earth holds some effect throughout the entirety of your energetic pathway. Unless there is recognition and a shift within and a shift around your consciousness.

Many of you who understand the nature of the mutilation of the feminine sexual organ understand and know latently, that this is what humans would perceive as an evil practice. For many forms of this around the entirety of the world takes away the ability for full sexual climaxes to occur. These beings are being taken from their sexuality due to the stigma and fear that a feminine sexuality incurs. And of course, as we go through our exchange in this way, we will, of course, touch upon this subject as well.

The masculine being, however, is not frequently seen as evil. It is frequently seen as a necessity for the cleansing, for the care for the religious order of that entity. And yet, although it does not take away all of the ability for the climaxes, or at least the greater form of the climax, with the construct of the removal of that skin, it still holds great trauma to the body, trauma to the penis, and trauma to the orgasm as a release and climax as well.

So in that way, a vaginal orgasm versus that of a clitoral orgasm with the clitoral orgasm removed. It is similar to the higher penile orgasm that can be achieved with those who hold their foreskin in full versus that of those who are removed. So in this way of course it does hold similar sexual trauma, although we understand your collective accepts them at a much different ability.

Both children who are taken into these co-created collaborative forms of energy and having sexual parts of their own anatomy removed all deal with initial forms of physical trauma and energetic trauma.

Both children who are taken into these co-created collaborative forms of energy and having sexual parts of their own anatomy removed all deal with initial forms of physical trauma and energetic trauma. There is an understanding innately from a child that its own mother will be the protector of that being as it has been for the previous nine months in utero. This bond becomes slightly damaged to broken in many cases when these energies occur.

This is why you see in more male-dominated societies with high aspects and populations of those who are circumcised, men that treat women unfairly, men that treat women as if they are nothing, or second-class citizens.

In the same way that in a feminine-related society, where a monarchical form of energy expressed through the elders are commonplace where feminine beings hold a great deal of sway and power, even if not directly in rule governmentally, in the villages where this occurs and these entities are expressed through that same term, the mother being related and the energy of the feminine consciousness is expressed in that way.

And in those societies, even when the masculine beings, are those that are perceived in charge. The feminine energies hold a very strong feeling of separation from other feminine beings and of course, anger towards the masculine counterparts.

You're already starting the journey after birth with a separation and segregation just from the first part of the birthing process and the rituals that humans have gone through for various other means. Sexuality could never have come to a place this wounded had the original sin not occurred.

In our own terms, sin is defined as your lack of connection to your own consciousness, to your Higher Fractal Consciousness and Higher Self.

As many humans who hold Christianity or Judaism to a belief hold and of course we would express that the only original sin is that of separation. In our own terms, sin is defined as your lack of connection to your own consciousness, to your Higher Fractal Consciousness, and Higher Self. To your own center of Source Energy and all of you have that initial sin at the beginning of your experience.

Now, of course, those who are not altered in any fashion, be it within the areas in which Western society have called themselves this, it is mostly feminine or female beings who are untouched in that way at birth. And for certain Central African and Asian regions, there are many of those feminine beings who are harmed initially as well.

So you understand and see the greater imbalance is upon both in societies that allow a sexual co-creation from a child without a consent, without an understanding, without permission, and with an indefinite and permanent harm that comes from the initial interaction as well.

Even when those humans heal in the emotional sense and start connecting with their body, regenerating energy in the fields of their own inner and outer healing, these constructs still occur.

Even when those humans heal in the emotional sense and start connecting with their body, regenerating energy in the fields of their own inner and outer healing, these constructs still occur. There are still forms of that pain that remains.

Now as we speak to those that are growing through children and childhood activation of sexuality comes early in human consciousness. Many humans who are within pre-pubescent ages still hold a sexual form of charge, even though it is not understood as such. It does not manifest itself in that same way, but it is often ignored by many other human beings until those cases of abuse in a sexual fashion occur and then it is expressed through those that had been abused and shared extensively.

It comes as a natural part of a growing body activated with more and more of their Higher Fractal Consciousness entering their body.

And of course, the energies that are creating sexuality in human consciousness do not come from birth trauma. It comes as a natural part of a growing body activated with more and more of their Higher Fractal Consciousness entering their body.

This is why you perceive those that are in the stages of puberty to be extremely sexual beings as they enter that part of their consciousness. If there was no birthing trauma, if there were no traumas related externally, which in our own experience with humans rarely ever occurs. But even with low thresholds of that energy and low amounts of sexual trauma being projected into those that are children as they reach the puberty region or age, then of course sexual activation occurs and can manifest in multiple ways.

One of the energies that humans understand and understand well is the nature of sexual orientation. In fact, you have sub-categorized it more so than what we would use for terms to explain these constructs. Now, there are those in our own perspective who are monogamous and there are those who are pansexual and there are those who desire sexuality with one group of humans and another who enjoy it simply with all groups of humans. These are the differences that in our own perspective are more so important.

Human beings who grow into their sexuality and have attraction for one sex or gender within your human collective are often expressed experience for the benefit of their family's understanding of a certain protocol that must be approached when it pertains to sexuality. We understand as humans there is the adage that humans create that expresses, "Of course, you will have those feelings for a girl because you are a boy. Of course, who will have those feelings for a boy because you are a girl."

This is that societal form of energy being expressed to the children who are of course looking at that adult in high level of excitement, high level of understanding, and a high level of praise from the child to that adult. So, of course, they will pay more attention to the sex in which they are told.

Some humans' energy fights this greatly. Some of those human consciousnesses hold that they prefer the opposite version of sex in which their family would choose for them. Now, of course, even in this factor, many humans still express, "I am a girl. I do not like boys and only like girls."

Yet it is still only one gender and sex for which this entity is showing compassion or connection or sexual feelings. Much of this can be concerned with fighting back against the programming the external world does to you.

In our own perspective, out of all humans that we perceive, there is a spectrum of bisexuality within each human being. This of course is extremely natural as all who had given their own DNA held pansexuality, bisexuality, or even that which was monogamous, but monogamous for creating children. And other sexual partners did not matter what specific sexual energy the being was. It simply shared love through sexuality.

So in that term, we see all humans holding a spectrum of bisexuality with a level of that energy being extremely high in one direction, extremely centered in both, or extremely towards that of their own.

So in that term, we see all humans holding a spectrum of bisexuality with a level of that energy being extremely high in one direction, extremely centered in both, or extremely towards that of their own. And each of these is not incorrect. Each of these is its own spectrum to that construct.

Now, of course, many humans who hold heterosexuality and the fear of homosexuality or bisexuality, these entities do in fact hold a greater resistance against that of the same sex due to the nature of programming. Even though there are humans who hold ninety-five percent toward one sexuality and can be a natural percentage of that spectrum, the five percent is thus ignored. The five percent is punished when thought about, when spoken about, or when projected into that construct of human consciousness. That energy alone will create resistance and will create a severing of that form.

Now as it pertains to the construct that we have shared physically as it pertains to transgenderism, the construct is very similar. There is a feeling internally that is identifying sexual components to be attracted toward a certain entity or a certain type of human being, whether it be masculine or feminine.

Now we understand not all entities that are transgender do only create with one sex, but more so than not. When they are connecting to that sex of their preference and are connecting with that construct of energy, they are also taking account of how they feel as an expressed consciousness. It is not simply bisexuality that holds the spectrum for the human collective.

Masculine energy and feminine energy are also a spectrum of human consciousness.

Masculine energy and feminine energy are also a spectrum of human consciousness. Some of you are highly balanced in a central portion of both. Some of you highly masculine. Others highly effeminate. But still, that ratio for yourself, if not twisted or molested externally by others' perspectives or forced upon your perspective externally, left to your own accord this energy, too, would show itself into the co-creative field as the energy of masculine and feminine in all human beings and the spectrum being adhered to by each person's personal spectrum, vibration level.

Now, of course, when you are feeling very feminine, but your body is extremely masculine. That energy of identity comes more so into that level of feeling feminine, not simply because it is a flowing form or natural construct, but simply because of the pressure weighed against you. You feel that greater form of energy underneath and subconsciously that expresses itself as the desire to be that of the opposite sex.

Now, of course, many Souls care for specific gender types, yet will attach their selves to a body that is opposite.

Now, of course, many Souls care for specific gender types, yet will attach their selves to a body that is opposite. To get into that family and get into that area of the earth and to get into the position where all of their experiences are held to a higher degree of probability and do so in taking the wrong sex body as what they desired. Many of those that are transgender, that have not had oppression of sexuality in one or multiple ways have not had pressure.

Masculine versus feminine fall into this category as well. Regardless of what arena your physical body takes hold, regardless of what your masculine versus feminine, regardless of your spectrum of bisexuality, human sexuality itself holds a great deal of healing capacity. Holds a great deal of interconnectedness of your own consciousness and the consciousness of others.

Whether it be the more animalistic, low chakra version of second chakra only sexual exchange, or whether it be that of the Soul connecting heart chakra sexuality, all of these hold levels of healing required for each individual human that is found somewhere within the spectrum of sexuality. Somewhere in the spectrum, masculine versus feminine, and somewhere in the area of their own tuned consciousness to the physical structure itself.

As we go into the physicality of sexuality, of course we must speak of mechanics involved physically in the act of sexuality itself. All humans that are aware and understand what sexuality is and what sex and the act of intercourse is itself understand and know that the act of intercourse itself is the form of sexuality most humans perceive sexually. But to those of you who are more explorative through different acts of sexuality, understand and know that intercourse is not the only act of sexual exchange that occurs.

As we go into the physicality of sexuality, of course we must speak of mechanics involved physically in the act of sexuality itself. All humans that are aware and understand what sexuality is and what sex and the act of intercourse is itself understand and know that the act of intercourse itself is the form of sexuality most humans perceive sexually. But to those of you who are more explorative through different acts of sexuality, understand and know that intercourse is not the only act of sexual exchange that occurs.

Some of you more studied in the focused arts of tantric co-creation and tantric forms and modalities of exchange understand and know that simply by holding one another and breathing together that you can create a sexual co-creation. That it can be as stimulating to the physical structure and the mind as the act of intercourse itself, or the act of sexuality of your preference of course.

Knowing that the energy of your consciousness holds the capacity for you to feel as nearly to the orgasm as possible without your body being involved, then you understand that sexuality goes well beyond simply the physical attributes and simply the physical mechanics.

Knowing that the energy of your consciousness holds the capacity for you to feel as nearly to the orgasm as possible without your body being involved, then you understand that sexuality goes well beyond simply the physical attributes and simply the physical mechanics.

The energetic mechanics are important as well. The feelings of sexuality, the co-creation of sexuality. And although we have covered a great deal of this, we will share how the chakras work with sexuality.

As you are engaged in co-creation of sexuality your chakras are moving at a quicker pace. You have more excitement.

As you are engaged in co-creation of sexuality your chakras are moving at a quicker pace. You have more excitement. You are letting more of yourself in if you are not resistant in your sexuality.

If you are receiving from the Higher Fractal Consciousness, this opens one of two portals majoritively, it opens the second chakra portal. The animalistic version of your sexuality comes forward. This is where you are having sexual congress that is engaged at high levels of physicality. Where the maneuvering that your body does becomes as important, if not more important, within the form of connection between the two who are having sexuality. Many of you hold one-night stands as the aspects of your sexuality, know animalistic sexuality because it is connection of the physical body stimulation, more so than that of the mental and the heart stimulation.

Now when we express the form of mental energy itself, this holds two forms of sexuality itself. The mental form of going behind your sexuality with thought. These lean within your animalistic side. But the mental body of connecting with thoughts as you are going to co-creation of sexuality can be either in the physical structural, or the emotional structure, the animalistic versus the heart-centric. And of course, the heart chakra being related to receiving and connecting creates the same form of sexuality.

There are humans in the world that do not understand and know that sexuality can be a greater emotional experience than it is a physical experience.

There are humans in the world that do not understand and know that sexuality can be a greater emotional experience than it is a physical experience. There are also those who do not understand the simple pleasures of the physical aspects or experience of sexuality as well.

In our own perspective, because humans hold a great deal of different energies within them, a great deal of the genetics of their ancestors, the iterations of DNA change it must come into the layers of their own consciousness and what is best for them. Some of you only can have animalistic sexuality. Others can only have heart-centric sexuality. Yet both play an important role in the human experience.

Understand the energy itself as it co-creates with the consciousness of other humans, this becomes a highly important level of intimacy for the beings that are human and simply their act of sexuality for the simple joy or procreation. As humans connect with other humans, sexuality holds a great deal of greater pleasure with your own species of human consciousness connecting.

Yet sexuality from the human perspective is experienced outside of human-to-human-only sexuality. When we express this we are simply speaking of bestiality. Although this is one portion of sexuality that is trauma-related with human beings.

> *When you were perceived as glorified pets, when you were perceived as livestock, when you were perceived as the cute counterparts of the Annunaki and they had sexual relations with you, it is very similar to humans who would have sex with their pets and animals.*

When you were perceived as glorified pets, when you were perceived as livestock, when you were perceived as the cute counterparts of the Annunaki and they had sexual relations with you, it is very similar to humans who would have sex with their pets and animals. Their cats and dogs and goats.

The only difference is the high level of sexual compatibility with organs of sexuality due to the nature that their own genetics were within you. And it would be more so akin to the feeling and experience of human beings having relations sexually with a human being, hybridized with an animal, more so than a human being having a bestiality with an animal itself.

Now, when we say this, it creates greater discomfort for the great amount of human beings, as it should, and we understand that when the sexuality of this type occurs, it is ALWAYS started from TRAUMA.

When a human co-creates with an animal for sexual pleasure, it does so because it does not feel it can be trusted by other humans or cannot trust that human. Human beings would rather participate with an exchange of conscious sexuality in both the animalistic sense and the heart-centric sense. The animal consciousness is more comfortable to these entities who participate in bestiality.

Yet if you were to look at humans having sexual encounters with extraterrestrial beings that were not the same as a human collective race, would this be any different? And, of course, in many human's perspectives, it would be greatly different.

There are parts of the human consciousness that express themselves in desire to have sexual co-creation with entities that they are meeting in astral projected states, beings that are within hybridized programs for the Gray alien races and the hybrid races such as the Yahyel and the Plahyel. And many humans who engage with thoughts of sexuality with those guides that they have heard, with the guides that they have co-created with, or with other human's guides that are represented in similar ways as ourselves.

What we mean is by hearing a message that hits greatly into the heart of the human being, it can open the sexuality just as when feeling sexually attracted or turned on to another being in general.

What we mean is by hearing a message that hits greatly into the heart of the human being, it can open the sexuality just as when feeling sexually attracted or turned on to another being in general. It can activate that energy from the heart to the animalistic portion of sexuality as well.

Now the ethics of this construct are left to all of you, but we will share that many humans believe that they are co-creating sexually with those extraterrestrial and extra-dimensional beings, but they are truly projecting a version of their own self that is bonding with that being in the way that they understand bonding can occur. And because bonding upon the most intimate levels through sexuality and physicality occurs between human to human in a very physical way then of course the construct is then projected onto that entity. So a version of that being can be created and sexuality can occur.

Now we are not saying that there are no sexual exchanges with higher dimensional beings in your astral projected state. But the majority of those forms of co-creation come from the higher fractal conscious layers of your Higher Self.

Now we are not saying that there are no sexual exchanges with higher dimensional beings in your astral projected state. Of course, there are many times in which this can be experienced, but it is not the human attribute that is fully involved in that co-creation. The majority of those forms of co-creation come from the higher fractal conscious layers of your Higher Self.

You are exploring and expanding into the higher dimensional self where the higher dimensional self is working with higher dimensional fractals of other consciousness through their own forms of sexuality.

All of these things are greatly considered a mystery to most human beings. But the feeling of sexuality itself in the physical form, the feeling of sexuality in the energetic form, the mechanics of that energy and physicality, and knowing that the sexual co-creation from human to human or human to extra-dimensionals exist as a part of healing for the human being. It is an important aspect for human consciousness to observe.

Now, of course, if we spoke simply of these topics, we could speak to you for many months of your time in order. But we understand with time being a limitation, these are the constructs that we wish to share for this day. So we will express to all of you, not only are you loved, but we give our love to as well. And we bid you adieu for this day. Adieu.

G reetings to all this is Aridif. We understand that all of you desired to share your queries. Co-create the concept of reflections throughout the co-creation that we have shared with you previously. But before entering these constructs, we wish to share two things that we have always shared. The first above and beyond all things that are expressed in this day, to know, feel, and to perceive that you are loved is of the utmost importance.

When two entities, separate and segregate from one another, share an emotion that is known or perceived or felt as love. Are truly shared with one another. This is an energy of co-creational bond but limited to the construct of conditional format in which it is achieved.

But you are loved shows the representation of all consciousness within the universe that is created from the source of love itself, the energy of consciousness that binds all entities in the universal co-created collective consciousness together. And, of course, if you do not feel love from another human. If you do not feel love from an entity to yourself, know that truly you are loved.

Secondly, we wish to express that this is our greatest excitement to co-create with all of you not only in this moment but through all moments of your linear time perspective. And, of course, you may begin with your queries at your leisure.

Thank you very much, Aridif. These questions this evening are related to the information and the process that folks have been through after the first transmission. It has brought up, as you predicted and suggested, a lot of feelings and insights and desires for integration from folks who are taking the course and people in the future who will be hearing this material as well and going through this process. So we greatly appreciate the opportunity to ask you on behalf of these individuals, some of these clarifying questions for your insight and wisdom.

Yes. Of course. And we wish to express our own excitement and our own co-creational gratitude for your own consciousness being at the forefront of the voice of that collective, albeit collective energy shines deeply within the co-created vessel of that co-creation as well. And we thank you for this.

Thank you, Aridif. The first question has to do with the expression of the chakras. As you're familiar with, humans use birth control. The first questions is, does the use of intrauterine devices and other forms of birth control affect chakras? And what impact, if any, does it have, these kinds of birth control, on the flow and operation of sexual energy in the physical and energetic bodies?

First of all, the energy of internal use for that of birth protection does not always block the form of energy, but the intention behind this construct is of great importance. For example, those in-uterine formats of birth control that are related to copper can help certain electricity flow and the electromagnetic flows to be somewhat better in some circumstances. But for those who hold great fear over becoming pregnant or having sexual relationship, turn into a long-term form of relationship, the fear itself creates not only a blocking of that additional form of energy, albeit slight, still a form of extra and additional energy, but also takes great level of resistance against both the second, third and fourth chakra.

The intention behind a vasectomy is the same construct. If a human being only desires to create a fear sensation inside of themselves at the thought of creating life from sexuality, without an exchange of understanding why for themselves it is important for them not to be pregnant, or not to create pregnancy with another entity then of course the resistance itself holds within the second chakra and for most humans relating to the first, third and fourth.

The lower four chakras are extremely tied together as we have shared previously within the human collective consciousness and sexuality is tied to all of these within one term or another. If the intention alone is to prevent pregnancy so that you do not create an experience in which others will suffer the energy itself coming from a place of love, instead of fear, it becomes much more potent and much less resistant as well.

Thank you for that, Aridif.

Yes, of course.

You mentioned in this transmission that many humans carry portions of guilt from the many different races that contributed DNA to modern humans. One of the questions that was submitted is whether it is possible for sexual trauma to be passed down to subsequent generations and to hold the trauma of your ancestors in your current incarnation. And if so, could you please share what the mechanics of that are?

Yes, of course. This construct of passing genetic trauma from the ancestor to the entity that you are, or the entity that you give birth to, and passing from yourself to them, of course, is what we relate to the construct of epigenetics. And epigenetics is in fact hard coding inside of the DNA that relates to trauma's resistances from the chakra and into the DNA format. And the mechanics of this are quite simple.

After the overlay of your chakra system exists inside of yourself and holds a similar to the same pattern of resistances throughout long periods of time, that energy then is transmuted into your cellular level. The saturation of that energy into the cellular level ties to the DNA.

Now understanding the DNA for all entities, not simply humans, but all entities in the universal construct are extremely sensitive to the shifts of energy and receive as a signal receiver all of the information that is being passed along to that DNA. Part of this is the environment that you are in. Part of this is the expression of energy in which you are around. And the greatest part of this is the chakra system overlay itself.

So if you hold resistance in one chakra majoritively and hold that resistance for multiple decades, then this pattern of resistance becomes much greater, and then it's passed down into your children's co-creative field internally by the DNA itself.

Now, of course, understanding that this energy is physical and genetic does not mean that it is a prison sentence for those who receive that energy. Most of the time the transmutation can occur through the simple acts of working with your consciousness, working with the techniques, allowing yourself to go through the feelings of that trauma in your younger experience and go through by healing that resistance form. All forms of resistance in the chakra centers are expressed directly through thought and emotion.

So if you create a positive psychology, if you create a resistance-free or nearly resistant-free arena from the greatest capacity that you are able in that moment, you are able to start transmuting that which is held in your DNA.

This means that when you have children of your own, then of course you do not pass the grandparent's form of that energy. You create some form, as resistance is present in all humans at some level. But, within the construct of how deeply devolving that energy was and how deeply less trauma that you hold than your predecessors, then, of course, you are able to then pass down to the child the greater form of least resistant possible epigenetics.

Thank you very much for that.

Yes, of course.

Aridif, why do Souls choose certain incarnations where they would take on certain difficult energies and dynamics knowingly? I know that these Souls can see the epigenetic line and the potentialities before they incarnate. Why would certain Souls choose that? And may I ask a follow-up question that comes to mind? I know a lot of kind of evolved Souls that are coming into the planet now to break some of that patterning. And is that something that they've experienced in other lifetimes or other dimensions and other realities. Breaking those ancestral trauma lines by incarnating into those lines or some other mechanism?

Yes, of course. We will answer your second query first as it is vital to the answer to the first query. And that is yes. You are correct. Many entities that have existed in the Earth incarnation cycle and that have done several lifetimes of sexual healing for the benefit of their lineage, for the benefit of the Soul, and for the benefit of the fractal consciousness in which they are, come back into the Earth incarnation cycle to families who hold some of the higher levels of resistance possible and do so to help transmute.

And as all of you are aware the systems that connect humans to one another are twofold. The grid system that is the most direct and exchangeable and, of course, the earth system. And by simply existing in a reality that is tied to all other Souls that share the Earth Collective Consciousness, you are passing one 7 billionth of your own consciousness to the rest of the humans in the world, as they are sharing one 7 billionth of their own energy with yourself. And the more humans who become connected to one another who transmute this form of energy, of course, can help pass that healing and spread that energetic field of transmutation to others.

Now why would a Soul come into the Earth incarnations simply to experience resistance from that lineage and the answer is just as multitudinous as the possibilities of those in which ways they can create or transmute the same form of trauma?

Most entities on greater scales and from larger and higher vantage points of consciousness enter the lineages that hold higher levels of trauma simply to experience having difficulty with their own sexuality and then finding a way to work through that throughout their lifetime or have an experience in which the transmutation is extremely difficult to test that part of their own lower fractal consciousness. Remembering that all Souls come into the Earth Collective not for happy life experiences. This, of course, can be of the greatest great for yourself and the greatest great for all around you.

But, the energy that is embedded directly within each Soul consciousness and is dictated by that co-creational experience with the Higher Fractal Consciousness and the Higher Fractal Consciousness working with the Oversoul is simple experience. This is why humans enter their incarnation and can be a murderer or one who is murdered, who can be a predator or a victim, or who can be one who helps others or one who needs help. These concepts are simply experiences to be had on that higher level.

Now, we understand the human level is not level. You will not feel or experience your life in the ways that your Higher Fractal Consciousness and Oversouls do. So, in that way, it is important for you to perceive the energy that you desire to overcome more so then why it is there to begin with.

Now it is important for you to understand and know the answers for that query, but to focus exclusively on that energy and to promote greater resistances due to that energy will only revert your progression. But what it can do is utilize that knowledge in knowing how, where and when to dedicate your consciousness to revert certain parts of your resistant forms of psychology and, of course, to transmute the chakra energies to align with the greater needs.

When it comes to your entire Earth expression, and especially as it pertains to the construct that affects most humans most frequently, the energy of your own consciousness is important to focus upon rather in the way that you wish to expand and grow, and not the way in which you are harmed or hurt by that focus. It will only revert to the story that is told to yourself that will keep you outside of your present moment. But acknowledgment in that moment brings a greater field and sense of energetic expression and possibility in multiple probabilities growing outward as well.

Thank you very much, Aridif.

Yes, of course.

Another question had to do - and you touched on this in the first transmission as well - is why do some women have difficulty experiencing vaginal orgasms? What is the cause of this? And is there a way to overcome any resistance around that so people can experience orgasms vaginally?

Yes, of course. With most entities that are within the feminine construct who hold the most difficulty in a vaginal orgasm versus that of a clitoral orgasm is one of two constructs that are within. One is very physical. One is very mental and emotional.

The physical attributes of that are the working of positioning of either the penis or whatever tool that is utilized for the benefit of that orgasm and creating the perfect form of angle, momentum, and repetitiveness. But, that energy cannot exist within the achievement of that orgasm without the first, which is the mental and emotional energy.

What is the first thing that humans understand about feminine energy versus that of masculine? Masculine form is projected outward. The feminine brings it to receive. So it is mostly humans who are uncomfortable either with their physical body, the mental body as they are engaging in sexual energy or the emotional version of energy exchange of sexuality to start with.

And, of course, the stem of all of those resistances starts back with the original construct in which we have shared. The reversion of energy in human growth and evolution, turning resistance into the most natural form. And, of course, the social forms that we have yet to speak of in your linear time are still a great part of this expression. So, as you hear the social format of energy in sexuality, revert the energy back to this moment and express the same query in that way.

The energy itself of receiving must come at a perfect comport with yourself in the most spiritual aspects of your consciousness, the physical aspects of your consciousness, and the mental and emotional aspects of your own consciousness. If it does not open in all of those ways through either the combination or the participation between all of these points and energies, then the physical body cannot receive the energetic co-creation with a partner or the tool in which it's being utilized.

Now, of course, masturbation versus sexual intercourse or the use of tools are three different forms of categories themselves. Masturbation holds that the majority of humans would utilize in the feminine form would be with a tool construct. But masturbation itself is an important construct. There must be a circuit that is tied between yourself and yourself. And that circuit is not direct or linear in nature.

The circuit starts from the heart energy, the love of yourself, the care of yourself. The reason why you are masturbating must be accompanied with the query is your heart in the correct place for doing so? Now, we do not mean that you cannot simply desire physical release and this is not good enough property in order to achieve. But what we are saying is if there is no version of love for yourself as an act of self-love to give you that experience of pleasure, then, of course, working as a simple functional body response will not nearly be as deeply interactive or possible to achieve that form of orgasm.

Then that heart must go to the solar plexus, your sense of self or persons, as it were, and understood that personal relationship with yourself and your heart. The personal exchange with that version of yourself that you know and understand with your heart. And going into the second chakra. This is part of where the physical attributes are. Are you comfortable in your body? Are you overstressing your physical body? Are you holding your breath or tensing your muscles too tightly? Are you relaxing in the physical attributes of this construct? And ask those queries connected to your heart.

And then your heart connecting to the root chakra. Do you feel safe in your exploration of that sexuality? Do you feel as if you are complete in that moment and belong in that moment. And tie that to your heart. And then from the root chakra directly reconnect to the heart and the circuit is created. When you connect all of the lower four chakras then bring that energy back into your heart. It gives you the circuit of masturbation capacity.

Now, when you are with a partner we explore this much more deeply in a future expression of our terms into the co-creation of orgasm and the keeping of energy. But we will express that when with a partner there must also be an evaluation of all four of those chakras. If you are able to connect your heart to theirs and connect the solar plexus with their heart and back to your heart, then you can create a circuit with them as well.

And, of course, the most important portion of that energy is complete acceptance from yourself to yourself and with your partner in order to achieve with the partners as well.

Thank you so much, Aridif.

Yes, of course.

Kind of in a similar vein. What advice would you give to those who are experiencing other issues around sexuality and orgasm that they would like to shift, such as premature ejaculation? Can you speak to the mechanics and cause of this?

Yes, of course. Now, for the masculine form, it is quite opposite as that of the feminine from the place in which energy exists. The feminine form is meant to receive in that way. And the masculine form is the portion of energy that projects outward. So, of course, the highest form of masculine energy is the leaking of their own energy outward or the holding of their energy to an internal place inside of themselves. The mental process of that premature ejaculation, impotency, or all other male forms of energy that exist within the energetic co-creation that feels as if it is dysfunctional, does not work in the way that you feel.

First, there's automatically disconnection from the heart. The first time that a premature ejaculation may occur the first thought is something is wrong with me. This is the first barrier to the next form of premature ejaculation and continuing on and on. There's a continuum of passion energy that continues to perpetuate your own self-disdain and your own self for lack of better terms hatred in some cases that are extreme. That energy holds a continuous circuit of negative energy.

From the perspective of yourself leaking, you cannot hold a positive charge within your battery if you are letting go of all of that energy. The emotions that you hold go outward. The internal dialog keeps you inward and you are not able to express that term properly. So, of course, the mechanical nature of the physical construct is working mostly with the sub-chakra region.

Now, of course, the seven chakras that all of you are aware. There are chakras that meet halfway between your major chakras and quarter chakras between and less and less going into thousands of chakras with your bodies. Most humans may understand this as meridian points. Premature ejaculation occurs when you are trying to receive your personality sense and your safety sense from your second chakra and there's little to no heart involved. And mostly this is turned to the self. Of course, it happens in engagement with other humans through sexuality. But normally it starts with a masturbatory construct.

There's a level of excitement that builds in the human body that is not released in various other ways, such as holding excitements and acting upon them in your life. I do not mean sexual excitement alone. The energy of pure excitement as it pertains to all things in your life can be acted upon. This helps that energy move. It helps the consciousness of yourself start easing slightly about and a radical form of acceptance of the self is highly important as well. If there's no acceptance to yourself from yourself for what you are doing sexually, what you are co-creating with others sexually, it only continues to repeat the process without creating the circuit.

Similarly, as we've expressed that which is feminine and holding orgasm with the feminine format there must be a circuit created. Starting at the heart. Working to the solar plexus. Connecting back to the heart. Going from the heart to the sacrum. Going back to the heart to the root, asking all the same queries that you would.

Now, of course, with both masculine and feminine forms it is important as we share more so about the energetic field of co-creation and reverberation that holds the sexual form of energy internally. And we will speak of this in your near future as well.

Thank you very much, Aridif.

Yes, as of course.

So anger is being triggered as you suggested might happen in some members of the course around the manipulation of DNA and impingement of free will by the Annunaki. What advice do you have for them on the best way to process and release that anger?

Yes, of course. First of all, you do not deny that anger. We understand as humans that many of you simply feel anger and then start feeling guilty for having felt that anger. Once you felt experience of over saturation, of the boiling forms of energy, the first and second, third chakras all tightening and exploding the energy that is within, of course, that energy becomes extremely difficult for humans who are working to better their own selves.

But it is highly important not to block that anger away. Not to hide from that anger. Not to simply try to avoid that anger. All of these are counterproductive for the processing aspects of your own inner consciousness and the energy through the chakra system itself.

Starting with the construct of self of release that only comes when the process is fully felt. Now, as many humans have expressed, as Rob himself has expressed through other exchanges with humans and as we would share to you, the construct of feeling the feeling is extremely important. Knowing why you are angry and upset. Ask yourself in this way what truly angers me about this construct? Most of you will go straight to the answer that your free will was infringed upon by a race of entities that had nothing to do with humans. Yet humans as you understand them would not exist had this not happened.

So, ask yourself again, is that anger truly the root of that expression? And of course, most of you in diving deeply into your inner consciousness can express, yes, part of this is the problem. But what more personally about my consciousness, my personality, or my life experience is close to that energy. That is more close to home and personal to my own self.

Most people will associate some act or action that occurred. Some of you who are masculine may express that when you are born you are circumcised without permission, and that itself was harmful to you. So it roots back to this incarnation.

Some of you that are feminine beings will go into your consciousness and ask yourself why was I never told about the over-sexualization of the feminine construct as I entered my puberty. To be so unaware and hit blindsided with the sexual aggression forms of masculine entities? Why was no one preparing me for this? It goes back to this incarnation.

All of the energies that are placed within that anger of Annunaki for most of you have roots tied more directly to this incarnation. Understanding why you are mad is extremely important.

Now, of course, regardless of the reason, the anger still exists and is, of course, for lack of better terms, perfectly reasonable for the human consciousness to go through that experience. Feel that feeling. Process that energy by asking the queries, then work to find what is within myself that can become triggered by these constructs and what is the ultimate truth of those constructs.

This is extremely similar to the processing that we would share with all humans that is vitally used in the ten-step process of belief system changing. And the reason why we express this tool is that it is extremely similar to the steps and processes that one would take. The recognition of the emotion. The triggering of the thoughts that came to you as you formed that anger. Then the deeper dive into the truth and the true nature.

Most of you will find the answer becomes extremely simple as it pertains to the construct itself. Most of you after several layers of deeper diving into your consciousness will find that it is a feeling of not being able to express yourself in the world. A feeling of not being under control of your genetics. A feeling of not being able to shift your consciousness the way that you desire. The remembrance of higher dimensionality and the control of the physical nature with which it comes. The feeling of being vulnerable and being human and all of the energies that were forced upon the human collective consciousness was akin to the version of rape that humans experience in this incarnation energetically. External forces come to your physicality and exert their dominance upon you.

And there will be nothing that cures that energy permanently as it were for the initial form of feeling. But the repetition of breaking down internally what is most close to you, what is most important and why it felt so distinctly hurtful to the heart at first, and why you can release. Much of this will come due to the process itself. And, again, if you work with the ten-step belief system processes through this and many other forms of the experiences that may come up with you with the co-creation of your sexuality, with the diving into your consciousness, and the processing of all of the things in which all of us are co-creating at this moment, it will give you greater insight into your personal reasons themselves. As, of course, each of you will have a reason that is slightly to greatly different from one to another as well.

Thank you very much, Aridif. We will make sure that we provide the ten-step process to all the members of the course.

Yes, of course.

So knowing that many of those on Earth have a galactic heritage in a linear time sense in the past, present, and future, and that many higher-dimensional galactics have the ability to move through time as we know it, is it possible that some humans who are incarnated on Earth now were also simultaneously the Annunaki and other forms? More specifically, the female Pleiadians who became the Annunaki?

Yes. Now, of course, this goes into the multi-platinus forms of consciousness that human incarnations may or may not take in what is perceived as previous or future incarnations, and of course, as it is understood and known. All beings that hold relationship with human consciousness hold direct co-creation in fields of greater Soul groups and Souls that are within the Oversoul collective families of course. As the Pleiadians in this day work with humans diligently due to their bond to humans from their sharing of that DNA.

Then of course it would be understood greatly that the Oversoul shares Soul groups and Soul families with one another. The same that is expressed for those that are reptilian in nature, the same that is expressed through those that are Sirian in nature, Arcturian in nature, and, of course, the Elohim and the Annunaki themselves. All of them highly linked to humans due to their shift of DNA and their changing of human DNA of course.

So, yes, the shortest form of answer to this query is yes, that some of you have lived upon both sides of this tale. Some of you incarnated as the Annunaki, whether it be in their first, second, or third iteration to human co-creation, or whether it was a simple pass and to go visitation for one moment of one time. It is extremely common for those who feel the greatest reaction to that energy to have been an Annunaki at one time or another.

Now, of course, as we shared previously, the Annunaki came in two majoritive forms of human co-creation. Some that truly loved humans in a way that saw them as, for lack of better terms, glorified pets in that way. And others deeply disdained for the humans to see them as nothing more than equipment.

And your reaction to the news at first arrival that these entities did, in fact, shift human culture, human timelines, and the human genome from the beginning of human as you understand humans to be in this day. The more likely the reaction comes from your own co-creation being in one of those two fields of consciousness that the Annunaki were.

Now, of course, this does not mean all of you were an Annunaki or all of you were active Annunakis that co-created with human beings. But remembering after leaving the Earth incarnation back to their own ship and back into their own race's co-creation outside of Earth, there were many entities throughout the entirety of the race who spoke deeply and passionately about both sides of that energy.

Those that came from the second iteration of Elohim understood human co-creation. And many of you have incarnated as Elohim previous to this time.

Now we will share that despite the co-creation of DNA there many races who work with humans on that greater collective level, that in their own expression as fifth and sixth density consciousness come into Earth's co-creational field to co-create within simply to change their own timeline. Now, of course, all of this is a bit jarring for the majority of humans. All of this recites and forms that original form of anger, angst, or question that arrives at your initial understanding.

But remember upon the Soul level all of you are creators first. Secondly, you are Souls that join for a co-creation. But many of you are not in the same timeline that you were one hour previous to hearing this consciousness.

Some of you are in drastically different timelines that existed one week previous to this co-creation, and much of you will be in a different place in one week from this time in the energetic field. And those of you who are focused in excitement in this co-creational field will continue to share your timeline.

But many humans divert. Many versions of the humans that you are co-creating with are true projections of your own consciousness, rather than that which is a focused form of co-creant from another form of consciousness. One that you would recognize immediately as another Soul. Another human. Another consciousness. An entity themselves. So all of the Souls that exist are interconnected.

And yet again, we understand the implication that from your human perspective, from your human experience, that it does not matter how deeply you are connected to a consciousness that is outside of your body at Soul level, at Oversoul level, and universal collective level.

If a lower fractal consciousness from another entity were to come into your space and try to infringe upon your free will, of course, there would be anger, there would be a fight back, there would be a repercussion. And of course, that is an important construct as to why you are co-creating within the first place.

Many of you who reacted in that form of anger are angry due to the nature of many infringements that continue to occur with you in this day. Finding boundaries between yourself and others. Finding internal boundaries with yourself. And the more that you feel the anger, the more deeply it is rooted in yourself and in the consciousness that either the infringement upon free will angers you because it occurs to you.

And some of you in very small percentages are angry because you are also infringing upon others' free will in some other form. You recognize that this energy is not a positive thing for the free will of another Soul. Yet continue to work with your own infringements upon others. This is extremely common in the

Earth Collective and at some level, most humans are doing something that will infringe upon some other life force.

Now, we have said this previously as you enter Earth in the co-creational field of consciousness it is extraordinarily important to remember that humans eat plants. Humans eat animals. Both of these are conscious, sentient energies. Both of these with a free will of their own. Animals eat humans in that way. And of course, understanding that they are sentient, just as you, but in a different format.

The human cycle, the human Earth Collective Consciousness was predicated that there would be infringement upon others' free wills. The Universe Collective Consciousness itself says that as the rule to start the Universe, to begin that there must be duality, that there must be two different forms of energy. That which is connected to love and wisdom. And that which is not connected to love and wisdom. That was the physical incarnation experience at its core. That was the agreement upon every fractal in a co-creative sphere.

And once you feel that sense of some form, it makes this answer, information, and conscious co-creation, slightly easier. But for most of you, it will not sit well until either the boundaries that you have not set upon those that continue to infringe your free will or the infringing that you are doing upon others comes to an end or comes to resolution through your internal self-consciousness as well.

I see. Thank you very much for that insight.

Yes, of course.

Aridif, thank you very much for this opportunity to ask you these clarifying questions. I know it's going to be of great benefit to those who are taking the course now and, in the future, to hear this. Before we wrap up for this session, I know you have the ability to perceive the energy of the Souls and the fractals taking the course so far. And I'm just wondering if there's anything additional you would like to share with them that might assist at this stage of the journey of taking this course to help. Especially those who for the first time are hearing this information and working to integrate the energy.

Yes, of course. First of all, the energy of what we have shared as a retort to the queries in which you've had or as an answer to those queries in which you've had are just as difficult in some ways or greater to hear for some of you. We understand this.

In the way of co-creating with other consciousnesses, many of those things that rub against your own self come from one of two places. Either the feeling that the energy itself holds some truth, but a feeling of resistance against that form of truth. Or something that is within you that feels resistant against that as being a part of your truth. And this is what we share with all of you who are going through that struggle as you hear the co-creation and the conscious co-creation of the entire collective.

And, yes, it is very important for you to utilize the internal feelings of emotion as a reflectionary construct. It is important for all of you to feel the level of intensity or the level of excitement that comes from the answers to each query.

The regulatory systems of the chakras are created in forms of humans to be extremely reactionary from the emotion and mental state. But the emotion starts the process. When you first feel excitement. When you first feel anger. When you first feel shock. There are all underlying reasons for that construct.

Processing of that energy is vitally important for all of you. Secondly, there are many of you who hold great queries at the moment of hearing this simply from what we have shared in this day and what we have shared previously in your first day of exposure to that energy as well.

But of course, there are many queries that will be answered forward as you go through. Many of the queries that some of you have held in this day will be answered at a later time in more complexity. Some of you that have queries will not be answered in that time as well.

But asking the query in iterations between collective forms of release that are shared in the format in which you are sharing is important for you to partake in. Especially if you are feeling excitement or feeling the opposite of excitement. Both of those are indicators that there is more to go.

When you feel disassociated or unattached to an answer, it is just because either you have worked through this construct already or that there's no need to work through this construct because it does not attach itself to your own personal growth experience. So remember when you feel that great excitement, when you feel that great opposite of excitement, ask your queries as to further the exploration of that energy.

And we do not simply mean by our answering alone. By asking the query, you are putting that energy into the reflective co-creation of all of our co-created field. By doing so, you will not simply receive our verbal answer back to yourself. You will hear the energy properties of reflection from one another.

All of you are deeply integrated with one another for the topic alone. And it is important that you are open to receiving the energy of others as well without judgment for how your reaction goes. Without judgment for other's reaction and with an acceptance for the queries you are asking itself. As all of the queries, whether you feel others may know the answer or not, are vitally important to be expressed verbally.

It is akin to those humans who are masculine who hold in their energy. Or akin to a feminine consciousness that does not receive. It will create that resistance of being stuck in your throat and heart chakra and often your solar plexus as well.

Ask your queries, be it to a public format to be reflected by ourselves, or ask your Higher Self the queries when you feel that excitement and when you are feeling the opposite of that excitement. It is important to speak to your Higher Fractal Consciousness regularly as it pertains to any of these energies that feel resistant or stimulating to yourself.

It is also an important construct that we share with all of you that although feelings that you have within the co-creation may be of opposite spectrum of that in others, or opposite of spectrum of what you yourself would have experienced years ago to hearing the same consciousness expressed through that reflection and iteration. But it is vitally important for all of you to be aware of what is going on within your own heart, within your own solar plexus, and within your sacral chakras, as these are the most akin to the co-creator fields the energies that we have shared in this day. As well as your safety and sense of placement in your first chakra.

We also wish to express that as we are reflecting that in which you are asking for the query, it is giving us that same form of opportunity to expand with all of you. We congratulate you for the growth that you are going through, and we thank you for the growth that you are giving us as well. We wish to bid all of you adieu for this day.

PART TWO · TYPES OF SEXUALITY THROUGHOUT DIMENSIONS AND RACES

G reetings all of you again this is Aridif. We wish to express greetings to all of you. We wish to express as well that we understand all of you desired to speak of the purposes and types of sexuality throughout dimensions and throughout density, throughout the construct of creational form and co-creational energy as well.

But before diving into these constructs we first express that, of course, above all things that are expressed in this day, to understand, to feel, and to know that you are loved in our perspective is of the utmost importance.

Secondly, it is our greatest excitement, and within that same great excitement in which we co-create with you, not only all of you as individual entities amongst consciousnesses that you are within, but also as a part of the co-created collective consciousness as well. The group of your energy, the entities that are directly involved in the co-creation as well as those indirectly a part of this co-created collaborative form of conscious co-creation.

Now, of course, we first express that as we are diving into these queries and topics, we must express that we understand through what is being shared about sexuality, that there is a great deal of trauma that is involved. Some of the subjects that are expressed within this time will hold traumatic effects in simply hearing the constructs that are involved within this co-creation. As we understand, just introducing the construct in our last co-creation, it triggered a great deal of anger in some, frustration in others, fears in yet others, and excitement in some.

Then, of course, from culture to culture, holding differences, the greater majority still holds trauma within the veins of this one construct alone.

Now, of course, all of these are par for the course as is expressed through your terminology for the experience of speaking of sexuality. Sexuality that is within the mainstream alignment of your understanding in the cultural niches in which they exist as well. Speaking of the topics in which are vastly niche and taboo, for your co-creative collective consciousness, yet all of them apply to the greater co-creator collective consciousness as sexuality has evolved through your species and through your history. Then, of course, from culture to culture, holding differences, the greater majority still holds trauma within the veins of this one construct alone.

This is why we have shared in the constructs of co-creation that we have and the ones in which we desire to do. So, of course, without further ado, we express that sexuality is utilized for human consciousness as means of two different forms. First, reproduction is what drives the mechanical nature and the chemical nature of sexuality for the majority of humans, even those who are leading with their hearts. They are still tied to the pheromonal, hormonal, and chemical constructs that sexuality creates within the body itself.

Now your second chakra's energy link and your heart energy link to the form of sexuality in which you are participating in of course co-creates the pheromones and hormones at different levels, at different intervals, at different quantities and different ratios of quantities per mixture of hormones and pheromones.

So it is important for all of you to understand that given the same sexual encounter with the same humans involved and the same co-creative form and feel of energy two different times within moments that are stretched from months to years under the exact same form, circumstance, the set of mind, the emotional contract, the energy that is within the context of that co-creation also will change all of these fundamental integers that we have expressed through pheromonal, hormonal and energetic arousals.

Of course, we speak to the construct of utilization for reproductive means in the human context. But yet another layer is added upon human context, and this is not abnormal as well. There are many races that engage not only as the larger part of that energy to create a thriving for the species in which they exist but also a very emotional, mental, and animalistic sense that is embedded within the construct of sexuality as well. Now, of course, there are some races that work only in reproductive form. And others that only work with a pleasurable construct of energies.

Now, of course, the main difference, as all of you will understand physically at the end of the act of sexuality for reproducing alone creates an offspring, creates the tying of two forms of genetics, and allows a body to be born from that energy. And, of course, a Soul will desire to attach to that body and then life is created.

Now, of course, this is not the only way in which reproduction occurs, but for humans, this is the standard form. The animalistic nature can be added to this construct or created separately with the ending result being the same. With the child being born and a Soul attaching to that physical body that was devised from two separate consciousnesses, holding their own genetic lineage, holding their own DNA, and holding their own energetic patterns, beliefs, ideologies, and epigenetics as well. Once two pairs come together as one in the act of sexual co-creation. Whether the intention for that energy is to create life or for simply the pleasurable interaction that it involves, that result of having a child can come nonetheless.

Those races that work for sexual gratification in their sexual exchange only cannot conceive birth from their sexual exchange.

Now, in different races, of course, this is much different. Those races that work for sexual gratification in their sexual exchange only cannot conceive birth from their sexual exchange. The organs that are attached to sexuality and be it drastically different from race to race and similar in many races are still not connecting with the parts of their own selves that are able to reproduce.

For example, TReb Bor yit-NE's race is a non-sexual. If they were to co-create in sexuality with their bodies and appendages slightly differed in order to form a penis and vagina so that they're exchangeable in that way would, there would be no sperm cells in the masculine form and no ovum in the feminine form. There would only be the appendages that are required and the entrances that are required for sexual engagement. And no children could come of that energy.

Yet we go to other races as example. With a race that is insectoid by nature. These entities are much to what humans would perceive as spider humanoids or spider insectoid beings. These entities do not hold sexual co-creation in an entering of the body from appendage to entrance with an exchange of fluids that creates a child. More so, the energy requires that which is the feminine being to create a sac within their own appendix region and within their own constructed body, a body is held in nearly full design.

The masculine entity would come through their own experience and their own tribes, be it sexual or reproductive alone, and create an entrance into that abdomen area with the final parts of the coding cell. And this would come from the tongue region. So in your perspective, it would appear as one spider licking the stomach of another and there would be the child in reproduction. From the entities that are insectoid spider humanoid consciousnesses.

Now, of course, this is radically different from one race to another. Yet many races especially that are humanoid in nature hold the same variety and combination that humans hold. Penis or phallic formed appendage for the masculine energy and an entrance or vagina for the feminine beings. Once those are co-created, then, of course, the sexual reproduction of a child comes to fruition.

There are some races that are humanoids that hold no ability to reproduce, but these entities once did utilize that for reproduction.

There are some races that are humanoids that hold no ability to reproduce, but these entities once did utilize that for reproduction. The evolution of their consciousness desired to start having babies in the same way that TReb Bor yit-NE's race would have children. To give samples of genetics from both parents create what humans would perceive as a protein-formed egg, creating a body within, and adding the genetics so that the body could form from the genetic lineage of both parents and then a child would be born within that area of the protein sac that was formulated by a scientist or from the parents with their own knowledge. And the Soul would enter the body in the same way.

Now these entities who desired to have children in this way, compared to the standard form in which they once had, all have different reasonings. But, because they are only handfuls of races that do this, the majority of them continue to utilize the sexual behavior for excitement alone, for fun alone, or for the merging of consciousnesses to create higher levels of intimacy alone. Sexual reproduction taken care of in another way becomes supervious to the constructs and energy of what once was for their race.

Now, of course, with that co-creation of having children in the new way, evolution breathes the need for the sperm, for the egg, and only creates internal versions of those energies. An organ that holds that half portion of DNA encodement within the masculine beings inside of their lower abdominal region. And for the feminine entity, a larger but equal and equivalent form of the feminine half of that genetic coding. And both are extracted, and both are given to this protein egg cell form.

Now, of course, they are not all eggs, and of course, they are not truly made of protein. But from a human level of understanding of the dimensionality, it would be the closest common construct that you would be able to perceive in similarity to your own in order to create such an experience.

Many races who hold this practice through their fourth density and fifth density, and eventually to their sixth density consciousness evolution, do so for the fact of their own physical bodies being that of one which they are loving.

So now, going back into the form of sexual co-creation for children alone. For reproduction alone. Many races who hold this practice through their fourth density and fifth density, and eventually to their sixth density consciousness evolution, do so for the fact of their own physical bodies being that of one which they are loving. One which they hold dear to them. One which they see as sacred and one which they see as perfect with no need to change the design.

And, of course, through the entire race evolving through fourth density entrance of the heart and fifth density, the entrance of wisdom, and sixth density, the entry of mastery, all of the energies underlined are not as needed or required. They do not have to concern themselves of what would occur with the co-creation being that of a messy dynamic or a separation or a divorce. They are simply emotional constructs that are no longer needed or required for races that have evolved to this level of consciousness.

And although many of those that are of Type Two nature who are that of the Type Two and semi-benevolent to malevolent, may hold certain attributes of separation. Or may hold segregation within their own race and problematic formats of parts which their own culture had not evolved throughout the entirety of that experience, the markers that indicate the growth of each race still show an appreciation of one another within their own race, a commonality within their entire planetary species, a love that forms for their own genetics, for their own selves, and for their planetary co-created collaborative form.

> *Once fourth density has been achieved and once fifth density begins, there are very few races who continue to strive with inner conflict.*

Once fourth density has been achieved and once fifth density begins, there are very few races who continue to strive with inner conflict. The mastery of the connection between one another has already occurred. Then it requires no further understanding of what the planetary consciousness means. And although, where the planetary consciousness goes from that point, of course, is explored in the next density.

But the way in which they treat one another, the way in which they perceive one another, and the way that they co-create through the rules, ideologies, varieties, types, segregation or not, they are still deeply appreciative of one another and the roles that are involved for the specific classes, or the specific groupings of the entities that are within their own planetary consciousness.

Most of the entities that are at a mid-fourth density level understand the nature of Oversouls. They understand the nature of the construct of the Oversouls grouping together to create planetary forms of consciousness. And whether they understand it by those terms or not, they feel what a planetary consciousness feels.

Now, you understand with the Earth Collective Consciousness, we understand the nature of division is quite noticeable in your experience in this day. We also understand that the idea of an entire world government is one that is terrifying to many humans.

So those who are sexually reproducing have already determined by fifth density what way they wish to further evolve and if it is sexual co-creations, the rules and ideologies of the entire species are already laid in the foundation.

But we would express that at this part of evolution at the end of fourth density, the entrance and the beginning of fifth density, are all co-creating from a consolidated energy of consciousnesses, a consolidated and agreed upon form of co-creation at a planetary level. So there is no division needed. So those who are sexually reproducing have already determined by fifth density what way they wish to further evolve and if it is sexual co-creations, the rules and ideologies of the entire species are already laid in the foundation.

They already understand if there are rules that you can only co-create from one class to another if you are only able to connect your family with another if you are only able to co-create with entities in your region or specific genetic markings. All of these rules are laid out differently from race to race but laid concretely in that place and region of time in which they are experiencing in which they exist. And this is what makes it quite easy for you to understand your place in sexuality once you have exited your fourth density experience.

Now humans starting at a detriment of consciousness...created a setback of thousands of years as we have shared previously.

Now humans starting at a detriment of consciousness, starting at a level that was quite well only two-thirds to three-quarters of the second density consciousness once third density started for you physically, this created a setback of thousands of years as we have shared previously.

But it does not mean that you will achieve living fourth density consciousness without starting to understand these things within yourselves. And once graduated know what your place is within the earth co-created format whether it be in handfuls of lifetimes in the future or hundreds of years in the fourth density in order to explore fully the construct of what it means to go through your connections in fourth density.

Now we flip the coin and go into the other side and look at those who co-create in a construct of only sexual co-creation for fun. And, of course, it is within similar threads and in similar veins of consciousness yet expressed quite differently through the densities that are the achievement of each race. Now, of course, as you understand the experience of non-child rearing, of simple satisfactory physical engagement and co-created fornication for the simple act of excitement alone. You can understand that there are many reasons for this to occur even on Earth and human standards. There are co-creations that are quite drastically different from human to human.

Some humans hold sexuality for the purposes of empowerment, of their own consciousness, of what humans believe their ego is and their own ego for the benefit of bragging rights, for the benefit of showing others that you are not a prude, for the benefit of yourself and for the benefit of where you perceive yourself in that experience of co-creating with other humans and your standard social standings with other localized groups of entities. And each of you has a purpose for the co-creation when you do not care what your social standing is in the environment in which you are.

There are very few humans who are sexually free and open, who experience co-creating with multitudes of other humans. Many humans who are emotionally well, who are intact with their own sexuality, who have extremely little trauma in their sexuality comparative to other humans, will sleep with less than one hundred other humans in their experience in the most part between ten and thirty-five.

Yet there are some entities who have gone over this construct, albeit unrealistic sounding to many humans there are, of course, many humans who have had sexual partners within the 150 to

500 range apiece. These are entities who are highly sexually active and highly changing partners at an extraordinary rate. And many of the entities who utilize their own sexuality in these terms are doing so as an overactivity in their physical body due to the overactivity of energy going to their second chakra. So they are utilizing it as their own way to express an overabundance of energy.

Now, of course, an overabundance of energy in one place - most humans perceive this cannot be a bad thing. And we express of course it is not a bad thing. It is only bad from that perspective of being bad.

The overflow of energy to your second chakra means that either your first or third chakra are also holding resistance and holding large enough portions of resistance that what energy that is not allowed to go through those chakras starts spilling back over into your second chakra.

In our perspective, the overflow of energy to your second chakra means that either your first or third chakra are also holding resistance and holding large enough portions of resistance that what energy that is not allowed to go through those chakras starts spilling back over into your second chakra.

Most entities that you perceive with the highest forms of sexual behavior are those who have places in their own safety that is damaged, that is feeling imbalance, that hurts their emotional construct. Or you have those who in the sense of their self cannot perceive themselves in a way that deserves to have love. So they are utilizing sexuality for the benefit of replacing love. They do not feel that they are worth loving or do not love themselves. So sexuality is the balance for them in that way.

Now, of course, there are some humans who can utilize this technique without it creating a form of further harm for themselves if they are able to work with that energy and, for lack of better terms, replace the forms of overabundant energy and siphon that energy into the place in which energy is hard to come through or hard to be a part of experiencing full energy through the chakras of resistance. Then, of course, it can help balance that entity. But most humans release the overabundance in sexuality through the orgasm itself.

Now, what we mean by this is as you are a masculine being this becomes more understandable through a visualization of the technique of your sexuality. While feeling the energy as it swells up within your second chakra you are stimulating the penis and testicles to a higher degree, stimulating the blood flow, stimulating the energy to the mind of excitement, and stimulating the entire body's chemistry. And the buildup comes to a greater place within their own self until they start feeling the edge and precipice of release.

And once they continue, whether it be through sexuality or masturbation, continue to work within the construct of that energy and finish their sexuality through climax of orgasm. Then quite literally the energy from their second shoots directly out in the direction of their penis out as their semen directly releasing that energy.

Now some humans who utilize either the feminine construct of energy of insertion or masculine beings who are taking the erect penis within their own anus structure and allowing sexual intercourse through the anus region are able to retain some of the form of energy that this masculine being releases during times of their orgasm.

And once this occurs, you find that many human beings who are feminine, or those who are masculine who are still interacting in sexuality with a masculine counterpart, but receive more than what they are giving. Are those who are higher in the grade of sexuality or in their sexual energy in the second chakra flow more so than those who are that of the ejaculation of men.

Now you understand the nature of masculine beings made specifically is a more wasteful act of sexuality in the way that humans experience it in this day.

Now you understand the nature of masculine beings made specifically is a more wasteful act of sexuality in the way that humans experience it in this day. Those who are feminine or those who receive that masculine ejaculation, these entities are getting the entire second chakra blast of energy through the entire part of their second chakra, third chakra, and heart chakra. They are receiving the portion of energy that the masculine being is giving away.

Yet those who are feminine construct beings who are achieving orgasm in that way of intercourse or clitoris stimulation their orgasm is one that radiates through the entirety of the body.

Now, of course, the masculine being still feels this orgasm the same way but the energy directs outward from the shaft of their penis out of their body. While those that are feminine radiate in the body and release from the crown chakra or root chakra and can sometimes release portions of that through the second chakra. But for the most part, those who have learned to relax with her sexuality receive that reverberation in the body and take more of that orgasm within.

Now, of course, there is a way that humans have invented long ago that allowed to keep that energy if you are that of an ejaculator or that of a masculine being who gives your energy outward in that way. Many humans who understand the nature of your history and look through the symbols of your history do not fully understand the symbology of those symbols throughout your history. For example, and specifically into the subject in which we have co-created with the ancient Egyptians, utilizing the symbol of the ankh.

What that symbol truly holds is the key to holding the vibration of your sexuality and of course, it works upon those who give their energy through sexuality or those who receive energy in the sexuality.

Now the ankh is one form of energy that was not meant to be a symbol of the gods and not meant to be the symbol of what entities upon Earth believed it is in this day. What that symbol truly holds is the key to holding the vibration of your sexuality and of course, it works upon those who give their energy through sexuality or those who receive energy in the sexuality. The masculine entity who ejaculates, or the masculine or feminine being who receives that ejaculation.

No matter who you are in that moment, you are able to take that energy and reverberate the construct within yourself. First learning to move your chakra energies is important. There are many techniques that we have shared previously, ones that Rob himself has shared previously, and ones that are written through multiple books that deal with chakra-formed energy, meditations, etc.

So once you understand how to move simply your energy from one chakra to the next, you will have a tool that is strong enough to work within this construct. And of course, the utilization of a visualization through sexual orgasm.

When you first feel the beginning of that wave that starts the explosion of energy from your sacral chakra, then envision the energy going instead of out your penis, or as the feminine construct allows that energy to go into their own body equally, perceive the energy going into your heart and you will breathe inward at that moment.

Allow that to sit within your heart for one to two seconds and as the ankh would show you allow the energy to go from the heart to the crown chakra in your breath outward. Allow the crown chakra to loop backward, both forward and backward from your body, into the very front center of your chest cavity into the heart chakra, and into the back between your shoulder blades and ribs to the back chakra.

If you were to stand sideways to another human and they were able to see your energy in that moment, what they would perceive is the symbol of an ankh, your head at the top of the ankh, your feet at the bottom.

If you were to stand sideways to another human and they were able to see your energy in that moment, what they would perceive is the symbol of an ankh, your head at the top of the ankh, your feet at the bottom. And the circular energy is that which released from your heart and which released from your crown and went back into your body. And that energy is the ankh in singular form.

Visualization of that energy of course is an important construct, as it will show you the way to hold yourself.

Visualization of that energy of course is an important construct, as it will show you the way to hold yourself. Now through the act of sexuality with partners, with two entities, one that gives ejaculation, one that receives that ejaculation of course this energy is much different. When you are working with two humans one that is entering the other it is preferable to either be completely at face to face or face to back, but be in perfect straight alignment as best as possible during the moment of ejaculation.

And once the ejaculation is given, then both entities perceive it going into the heart of that which receives and from that heart going out up to the crown chakra, releasing back into the loop, going back into the back portion of the heart of the giver. And into their own back into the heart of receiving and allowing their hearts to connect.

This requires not only visualization, not only two entities that understand the movement and nature of energetic movement, but it will also require two consciousnesses to hold love for one another.

Now, in this term of love, we understand through human sexuality, it often requires two entities that have given their lives to one another. One that expresses monogamy in the terms that they understand or expresses exclusivity. That I will only love this entity. We are not speaking of that form of love. This is a very human standard of love.

What we are sharing is a great appreciation for the Soul of this consciousness at minimal. A great appreciation for the moment between one another. A true caring of the Soul and not of the person or personality it holds, not of the entity that is in front of you, that is giving you sexuality in co-creational exchange. But truly a Soul that you hold dear and great love for. This is where in the couple form of holding the ankh reverberation of orgasm and sexuality. Then, of course, it becomes the most potent form of receiving through sexuality.

> *The only form that holds stronger energy exchange, reception, and reverberation than these is when that same couple is able to learn to have a climax together.*

The only form that holds stronger energy exchange, reception and reverberation than these is when that same couple is able to learn to have a climax together. And doing so both of them perceive their own energy going into their heart and redistributing to the other. And doing at the same time holds twice the effect of that in the singular. We have expressed this construct within the ankhing to show you the example of what non-child rearing sexuality can be among humans.

If you are looking at other races such as those that are Arcturian entities, they are quite literally creating an amalgamate form of their own physicality, linking bodies together through their own sexual organs and creating one entity between the two of consciousness. And of course, eventually a physicality.

And although they are reproducing, in some instances the majority of sexual co-creation is only for the benefit of extreme forms of connection to one another, an intimacy level that cannot be achieved in other means. When they are linking bodies and becoming one with one another, they are truly forming a bond that is higher than all forms of human love.

Now we understand human love holds one of the greater capacities for the ability to love, but becomes mired with desire for you to perceive that other person in the way that you desire rather than that in which they desire. This is done so with the greatest forms of love to children. This is done so with lovers to one another. This is done so with parents and family and holds capacity for a pure sense of love. But in these terms, this shows you an extreme form of two consciousnesses co-creating through sexuality and truly bonding with one another.

In other races, there's meditation where two consciousnesses link, and astrally connect with one another's consciousness through acts of sexuality, per their own race's sexuality or per their own race's physical structures that create from sexuality.

In other races, there's meditation where two consciousnesses link, and astrally connect with one another's consciousness through acts of sexuality, per their own race's sexuality or per their own race's physical structures that create from sexuality. Even that in non-sexual consciousnesses merging constructs have been created to simulate a form of what sex once was for their own race. Now, of course, not only are there those who reproduce, not only are there entities who co-create out of that of pure love but there are those that are asexual in nature.

Now, of course, humans hold a sexuality or non-sexuality within their own race. But in other races you see so such as TReb Bor yit-NE's race these entities hold no sexual organs. They reproduce outside of their bodies. They perceive one another as equals amongst their planet, yet they hold one mate, a genetic match, a Soul that feels slightly more connected than the rest. And they create children through that energy that we have shared previously.

But when it comes to the act of sexuality, there are no sexual acts that are involved. The feelings of intimacy with one another are equal to masculine and feminine forms from love of the child and parent showing absolutely no regard for the difference in your child's experience to a stranger that you have never met.

But you know because they come from your collective. They are deeply bonded with one another but hold no significance of family more so than that of the genetic lineage and that of sharing genetics with the other entities. And although they can group around their family or live near their own family, it is not something that is required.

The children are released from the laboratories in which the eggs are created and the child walks free from its own free will and volition. That being is able to walk years many times before meeting their genetic parents. And there are no qualms with that. There are no problems that are held within the mental, emotional, or spiritual state of any being upon that planet for that purpose.

The children are left to their own accord because those children will be loved by all, just as fiercely and as deeply as those of the parents of that child. So, of course, it is quite a different race, with quite a different rule for sexuality and part of the sexual co-creation experience.

But for all intents and purposes, TReb Bor yit-NE's race that which are affectionately and notably called the Yits per your human understanding and the nickname that is given by Jefferson within your human collective consciousness.

Now in the terms of humans, many humans do not discern or determine the differences from those who are asexual, from those who are non-sexual. But to our own perspective, it is quite different.

Those that are the Yits are asexual in nature. Now asexuality takes an entirely different meaning than that of human consciousness. Now in the terms of humans, many humans do not discern or determine the differences from those who are asexual, from those who are non-sexual. But to our own perspective, it is quite different.

Those who are asexual hold no interest in sexuality co-creation with other entities or do not discriminately hold a sexual preference for entities that are co-creational part and prefer to be alone within their sexuality. They cannot reproduce asexually, but they are able to take that fluid of reproduction of sperm and utilize it and self-impregnate. And of course, that can be an asexual birth from certain human perspectives.

But asexual humans in our perspective hold a level of sexuality. And although sexuality often does not excite them, often there's not a great deal of energy that is spent upon sexuality, there is still sexuality within them. Where those who are non-sexual hold zero interest of sexuality altogether. They hold zero desire to hold sexual exchange with themselves or other human beings.

Now, of course, both of these are not necessarily a consequence of sexual trauma in a direct way. Meaning not all asexual and non-sexual beings have been hurt, molested, or groped in that way.

Many of the humans that work in this are epigenetically hurt and epigenetically traumatized in their sexuality from an experience of their own family lineage of sexuality.

Many of the humans that work in this are epigenetically hurt and epigenetically traumatized in their sexuality from an experience of their own family lineage of sexuality, or the world's conditioning of sexuality, or the sensitivity level of that consciousness knows that to engage upon human sexuality takes a great deal of their own internal and external energy to participate in.

But simple participation alone in human sexuality automatically creates further trauma as well. The need for others to find you sexually attractive. The animalistic instinct that desires perpetuation of your entire species and done so through that animalistic portion of your sexuality. The construct of knowing that if your sexuality were to engage at certain levels, that a relationship can be held or destroyed through sexuality alone.

Now, of course, those that are asexual can desire, as can those who are non-sexual desire intimate relationships. That is part of being human. Most humans desire this. But they also understand that with a majority of human sexuality will be a part of that energy. Which keeps them from working with others, or only allows them to co-create and look for other humans who feel as they themselves do.

Asexuality itself is a part from a Soul level of the investigation of self-love, the investigation of being okay to be with yourself.

Asexuality itself is a part from a Soul level of the investigation of self-love, the investigation of being okay to be with yourself. Often Souls that experience this experience have gone through many forms of relationship traumas in their recent past incarnations and desire not to need to go through it in this experience.

Those who are nonsexual are often more traumatized than those that are asexual in their previous incarnations. These are often the victims of severe sexual traumas, such as those that are rape, such as those that are incest, such as those that are sexual torture. But this does not mean all of them are. A great majority of them are, of course.

But, of course, there are those humans who experience that energy and create hypersexuality so that they are able to experience sexuality at all terms and positive ways. You see this with many masculine forms and some feminine forms of those who have been sexually hurt and harmed, where resistances around sexuality were to be built up in other humans and it would turn the opposite for themselves. They would become over engaged in sexuality or have unnatural forms of interest in certain aspects of violence and sexuality.

> *In our own perspective, all things that are part of sexuality are built around either resistance or freedom of that sexuality.*

Now, of course, when we express the terms unnatural, what we mean is natural to the way that humans perceive the construct of sexuality. In our own perspective, all things that are part of sexuality are built around either resistance or freedom of that sexuality.

Some humans hold very strong levels of what other humans would say kinks that are within them. Those strange forms of sexuality that are taboo to the majority of other humans. And these entities can be some that hold the least resistance in sexuality.

Yet others are holding such great resistance in their own sexuality, they are trying to overdo the sexuality. And, of course, this is extremely personal from one person to the other. And one cannot fit within the other with the construct of what is the reason behind this specific desire to have strange forms of sexuality.

Now, of course, we have spoken previously about that which is unnatural from the human perspective. Those who work in bestiality, those who work in rape and violence, those who work in sexuality, necrophilia, and all of these extreme forms of sexuality, these are experiences from a Soul level that are needed experiences from a Soul to have an extremely off-putting, extremely taboo and extremely and highly charged sexual form.

Most humans who go into these forms of sexuality hold severe mental experiences of trauma.

Most humans who go into these forms of sexuality hold severe mental experiences of trauma or severe, as humans would call, mental illnesses, as we would express consciousnesses that have been fractalized through severe traumas, epigenetically, chemically, or direct experience can create all of those. But these are on such a far end of sexuality we will not speak greatly about the subjects alone. Although we have covered bestiality in quite a large spectrum, we will engage from retracting from these constructs for the moment.

Understanding and knowing the part and parcel of the energy for what is normal in human sexuality to our own perspective is less important than understanding the co-creational form of sexuality. The reasoning internally for one human to express their sexuality and what part of their sexuality holds resistance from their belief systems, from their mental bodies, from their emotional bodies, from the epigenetics of their ancestors, and from traumas that are related in this current experience of life.

We will express as well that during the form of sexual engagement that humans hold, there is quite a level of difference in the way that humans experience that same form of sexuality versus another human who holds the same form of position, the same energetic field, as we have alluded to earlier in this co-creation.

We wish to express to all of you that we will continue the query of sexuality and trauma, the forms of sexuality, the co-creations of trauma that come from sexuality, and a myriad of other topics. Especially in that of what sexual trauma is, of what variety, types, and kinds that humans often and most frequently deal with. And, of course, although we have touched upon this in this day, we'll dive more deeply in the next.

And, of course, the most important portion of this energy in our sharing of co-creation is how to work to heal the traumas of sexuality. As we understand the nature of sexuality and its resistance to each human is that it creates the very heaviest forms of resistance in the majority of humans with themselves. And the greatest form of divisive co-creation of resistances between humans and their counterparts or partners, lovers, husbands, wives, etc.

Whatever dynamic between two or more humans that is created through sexuality, sexuality and your trauma invested in that sexuality, is the greatest form of resistance between that dynamic and between those persons that are involved in sexuality as well.

We will express to all of you that we are experiencing the construct of sharing the energy and all of you reflecting upon the information internally, listening to your body in what part what we share activates what within yourself. We learn from perceiving you co-creating with our reflections and grow from that experience.

We wish to congratulate all of you for growing in this co-creation, and we thank you for the growth that you have shared with us as we are all truly connected and one with another. We will bid you all adieu for this evening. Not only are you loved, but we love you as well. Adieu.

Greetings to all this is Aridif. That is A R I D I F. And this is it spelled. We understand that you desire to speak of the queries that were produced from the co-creation previous of our own expressing the constructs within your first two portions of the four portions of the co-creative course collective consciousness. And we understand within your queries you learn a great deal about your own consciousness as well. Reflecting with the co-creative collective consciousness.

Before diving into those queries there are, of course, two things that we wish to express. The first above and beyond all things that are expressed in this day, to know, feel, and to perceive that you are loved from our perspective is of the utmost importance.

Secondly, it is our greatest excitement and within that same great excitement in which we co-create not only with all of you as a collective consciousness, not only each of you singularly, but as a co-created form of collective consciousness within co-created material at work with the collective consciousness in this moment and through all moments of your linear time perspective.

So, of course, you may begin your queries at your leisure.

Thank you so much, Aridif. We greatly appreciate the opportunity to share these questions with you so we can receive your perspective and clarification and wisdom on them. Thank you so much for your willingness to continue co-creating this course as people are moving through it.

Yes, of course, it is truly our greatest excitement.

The first question from one of the course members says at the time of the sexual act, if the chakras are open, there is usually an energy exchange happening. When a man ejaculates inside of a woman, does the woman take on masculine energy or the man's traumas, thoughts, and beliefs?

Now within this construct, there is a great deal of different energies that can exchange. And, of course, we share this in greater depth along the course of your future timeline in the next course and two portions of the course.

But, if you're looking directly at the receiving of that ejaculate form of the masculine being does not mean that you will take upon the resistance and wounds of this person. Does not mean that you will take on the traumas that are related with the entity. Nor does it mean you will take upon their masculine energy and insert that into your own chakra field. But, there can be aspects of this that are exchanged depending upon a great deal of circumstances and, of course, pending the co-creative form at hand.

The first is that when you are working with co-creator collective form between two entities alone, you are still working at a five perspective of conscious exchange. You are working with the person that is exchanging with you and yourself as entities upon yourself. You are working with the projected version of that other person across from you and their projected version of yourself. And then you are working with that collective form.

Now, of course, this does not entail or include all aspects of sexual exchange, but it comes to certain energies such as trauma relations and exchanges of that energy. Then of course there may be, for example, if the person across from you is projected to be by yourself a much more intact person, as it were, with their emotional and mental state than what they actually are in their own perspective. Then, of course, your own perspective would keep a great deal of that resistance out of your own energetic field.

And when you are working with the construct of seeing this person as a projected version as an extremely masculine entity whose presence of masculinity alone shares that energy upon all then you may be in higher percentage opportunity to receive that form of masculine energy. But, natively, it is only those who are exchanging with one another who hold a great deal of emotional, mental energetic imbalances and belief systems that are oriented with how much of their baggage must be exchanged.

We understand we have shared previously that any exchange of energy is an amalgamate form of co-creation. And, of course, this can be true for the human collective consciousness as well as the co-created field between yourself and the five persons energetic point of co-creation.

But with human relations, it is more so chakra energies that are exchanged. Whereas if the resistance to one party is given from the masculine to feminine. That resistance alone will not simply pass down the energies that are abundant, the energies that you would need in your experience to help fulfill your own energy deficiencies would be passed and more readily available.

But, if both of you hold similar resistances, it would give an average form back to both of you. For example, if one holds twenty percent resistance in your root chakra and the other eighty percent, you would create that form together and split the difference after the addition form. So, of course, this energy would be much different than if both of you were exactly the same level and then tend to balance out more deeply.

The only energy in that moment that is exchanged is the one that you hold available to you in that moment. If you are giving all of your emotions to another person. If you are willingly receiving all of the emotions of the other person, then you will receive that emotion regardless of the state in which it comes.

But, if you are simply enjoying the act of physical sexuality, then the energetic properties become secondary as a nuance rather than that of the primary focus of exchange. Therefore, any form of deficiency would not be spread as easily, nor would the form of masculine energy.

Now, if there are two entities that do not know one another at all and hold a great deal of resonance with one another, then both a masculine and feminine form would help balance out the other and the energies that were deficient in one another but strong in the other would, of course, help to balance those entities.

It is only those who hold great deals of imbalances, those who do not care much for one another as human beings, but still co-create in sexuality, or entities that have been traumatized together through their sexual experience in repetitive co-creations that would tend to be affected more so.

Thank you very much, Aridif. I know that you speak much more specifically about this transference of energy in later transmissions in the course. So thank you very much for that answer.

Yes, of course.

Another individual shares that her partner has had his prostate removed due to cancer. He still experiences orgasm, but there is no ejaculate. Will the ankh technique still apply and work if he has no ejaculate?

Yes, of course. When we are expressing the term ejaculate, it is more so for the sake of understanding the protruding forms of energy. If there is an orgasm, then the ejaculate is not the seminal fluid but more so that of the energy that is burst in release from the second chakra through the penis and out into those who are receiving that energy.

Thank you very much.

Yes, of course.

Another individual asks or really starts more with an observation and says some menopausal women start disliking sex because of various reasons, such as extremely heavy, painful, and prolonged menstruation, fibroids that might develop, and vaginal atrophy. They add that this can impact relationships as well as women's own mental and emotional health. Could you speak to why some of these issues manifest during menopause and how you might suggest positively working with them to reduce discomfort and possible negative effects?

Yes, of course. First of all, as you are perceiving menopause from that of a feminine entity and perspective in what is perceived by the Earth Collective as western forms of society, there's most frequently not a celebration of graduation to that energy that is deemed to be the crone in that of your ancient philosophers in that of your entities perhaps that most humans would express to be pagan in nature, but the energy that it relates to the consciousness behind the graduation from the early form of childhood into the womanhood and womanhood into the elder form of consciousness and then to the graduation of the extreme form of elder.

These are much different in their energetic properties and forms and cycles in the feminine energy itself as it were expressed. For example, the energies that are related to that of childhood hold a great deal of innocence, but also a great deal of working towards the construct of how to create, build, and form relationships as it becomes prioritized within the form of mental and emotional state and, of course, societal state will also play a part of this greatly. And into the puberty regions of your life cycle. Then it starts becoming an exploration of that blooming form of energy. It would create more complex forms of relationships.

Find what it is to feel manipulated by others, working towards the form of opening oneself to the experience of sexuality, onto that of the full form of adulthood and in to the region of life in where you are at in this moment, where you are going through the construct of menopausal forms of energy for those who experience this.

Now, if it were a celebrated construct. If it were seen as a beautiful graduation as once it was, the energy of the person independently, as well as the collective consciousness would not feel a larger effect of that energy.

Now, of course, the physical body itself holds a deterioration as time goes through. We have shared this in great detail in other places, as well as sharing the construct internally that as you are aging your cell reproduction becomes less. Hence, your own technology, as you were to make a copy of a copy, of course, that copy becomes degraded as time goes through.

And that is how your cellular levels work as well. And with that consciousness that is not celebrated and with the cells that are also making copies at the moment of that cellular reproduction, depending upon the person's energy, it will create either a slightly degraded form or a greatly degraded form.

And because humans are experiencing great deals of stresses and resistances through the parts of your own sexuality, the parts of your physical body that are directly related with your sexuality are starting to move in that direction. This is the same reason why masculine entities in their elder ages become connected to the construct of impotency as well. The construct of that cellular forms being not celebrated, not appreciated, not perceived as worthy in a greater sense.

Now, of course, the independent thought process helps greatly in this way. You understand the nature of your own experience. You understand your worth as a human being. You understand the infinite forms of wisdom grown in that time being exponentially much more than previous parts of your own experience. Self-celebration is in order in that way.

But even if you are working towards that construct, you are still working against the lifelong programs of sexuality and societal energies that we have shared previously and into your linear future that work against that construct as well.

Now the moment of energy that creates both physical resistances, with atrophy, with fibroids, with inability to work sexually as frequently due to the form of being able to hydrate and moisturize yourself in that way and lubricate yourself in that way being the same as previous. We understand the nature of this causing resistances between that of the masculine and feminine forms when in contrast to one another where one holds a sexual drive and another does not.

Now, of course, this construct itself holds many different energies. But they are more mental and emotional energies for the reasons of not desiring certain sexual for the majority of humans. Now we do not mean you yourself specifically. Nor do we mean that you are working within the construct of this layer, but for most entities at this time, it is their own disapproval of that transition into menopause.

It is that feeling that you are not appreciated any longer. It is the missing part of yourself as in the maiden construct where you were praised for your beauty, etc., that did create a form of missing that energy.

Now, we understand energy between the masculine appreciation of the feminine form and the feminine energy itself can drastically differ. There is appreciation for the feminine form from the masculine entity and that can create forms of resistance in the feminine entity as they do not wish to be sexualized, or objectified.

But there is with a person or people that you love most greatly a great form of appreciation of their recognition of that beauty.

And even despite many humans having a masculine counterpart that produces a great deal of praise for the entity themselves do not feel. They are feeling more so the societal disapproval of that growing into that age group and growing into the post-menopausal energy and emotionally and mentally the energy sets to the forms of imbalance more so than that of balance.

What you can do to work through this construct is open the dialogue between both of yourselves in the most honest and transparent way. Now we understand the nature of saying this alone about sexuality with one's partner is terrifying for many of you. There's a great deal of understanding of thresholds for your partner of sexuality. The differential nature of one partner versus another. And this alone causes a great deal of resistance for those who are in long-term relationships, and especially those of monogamous long-term relationships.

But within the transparency of sharing how you are thinking, how you are feeling, what you desire, what you are missing in your experience, and what you desire to give the other. And hearing in the interpretation of their own perspective without your judgment upon them, without your projection of what you believe they are saying, what you believe they are thinking, or how you believe they are feeling is vital.

We have shared previously the five persons perspective. That of the projected version of your partner and that of your partner itself. You must not allow yourself to project onto this entity while you are listening to them. Just as they may not do this to you as they are listening as well. Now once that communication goes into the construct of openness, and once the communication flows, there's a greater opportunity to start healing.

Now some of these energies will not simply go away. There may still be atrophy. Now we understand there are many exercises that can be done for this. But, there must be a participation with the partner as well. There are many things outside of sexual intercourse that partners are able to work with within the sexuality construct that will help bring healing to that energy.

Now, we understand there are many different forms of exchange of sexuality, human relations, and the co-created form. But it must be an experience of giving that feminine entity what they desire to help allow their body to become more comfortable. There must be given to that feminine entity, the energy that they need without forms of judgment, to help allow the body to start healing in that way.

And when the healing starts occurring in that construct, then the energy of sexuality for the other portion of exchange can be created more equally. So continuation of both conversations and looting from that conversation the energy that is required for the healing to begin.

But, you must also hold that self-judgment into your own processing. You must understand the level in which you are judging yourself for being at that age, for being at that mark of life, for allowing the co-creation of societal structures that are there, that place value upon certain age groups and energies, and devaluate the constructs that are opposite of this and must place your own value marker upon. The less that you judge this within yourself the more so you'll be open to forming a new experience of co-creations as well.

Thank you so much, Aridif. That is such a powerful message and I know you touch on that much more deeply further along in the course when talking about societal programming and how that impacts people's sense of self and their sense of value.

Yes, of course.

Speaking about honesty in connections, you discussed in phenomenal detail how sexuality is expressed and experienced throughout creation and at different density levels and through different races, which was exceptionally helpful to hear about and expanding of the consciousness.

So in a similar vein, talking about the preferences and various levels of excitement, one of the questions is how can Souls satisfy the excitement to have sexual experiences with various beings of various excitements when in a loving, monogamous relationship that isn't sexually as compatible?

Yes, of course. First of all, the energy that is related to this consciousness can be perceived from multiple levels. Now, first of all, as you are perceiving this construct there are multiple levels that are involved. The construct that occurs within your own desire to co-create with that that is your guides, with that that are Soulmates in higher forms of dimensions, with that of co-creative fields between the consciousnesses of yourself and entities that do not exist in your own dimensional form, in most individual perspectives are quite different that of the co-creative energy in your physical presence.

For example, the entities that are directly co-creating with you in forms of sexuality that are human counterparts are able to physically engage with your physical body in the dimensions in which you exist. And, of course, the exchange of that is quite physical.

Entities that exist within the higher forms of dimensionality will most frequently only come to you as you are perceiving your own astral projected form, meditation, or astral projected form of your sleep state consciousness. Now, within that energy, there are many different forms of co-creation energy. And we share more deeply at a later time some of these energies. But we will quickly touch upon them.

Most humans who are in co-created forms with guides, entities, and beings that exist are working with a portion of themselves in their higher dimensional bodies as well. That energy is an entity unto itself that you are specifically part of. Now, of course, this does not make sense to some of you. But, if you were to perceive it in a different way.

Imagine yourself as a worker. Imagine yourself as a family person. Then imagine yourself as a friend. There are three different roles that you play. But you are the same person. The same is expressed as your higher dimensionality, fourth, fifth, and sixth density versions, that are within Higher Fractal Consciousness, that are fractals of their Higher Fractal Consciousness. Even though the sixth density portion holds the fifth density, fourth density, and third density version of itself. Meaning you are the smallest part of that greater energy.

And the same that is expressed with the fifth density. Where the fourth and third remain within. And the fourth density version the third density exists within it. This means that once your focus has shifted into that dimensional form of yourself, the you that is you is only a small component of that energy. There is a much greater compatibility with higher forms of consciousness and your own Higher Fractal Consciousness because they are the same dimensionally, because they are co-creating from a field of a spectrum that is much wider.

So in that way then you're having sexual exchanges in dream states and your astral projected meditations. Of course, your own part of the energy is part of that co-creation. But a much greater part of you is also part of that experience.

There is not often a time where your own free will takes focus at that moment because your own free will is different in your physical body than it is in the higher dimensional format. And that is because the higher dimensional format perceives consciousness from a level of consciousness that it experiences these co-creations with.

A sixth-density entity would perceive the construct of a monogamous relationship to be an experience to be had and nothing more. It would not take it as a contract in which it may only have co-creation with one other Soul.

Now, of course, sexuality is not always exchanged in the moments that you perceive sexuality as well. Many times it is a Soul co-creation that is a bond of heart to heart. But in your own way of perceiving, translated into the most form that you can perceive and appreciate. And that is through the form of sexuality.

As when you feel a great sense of love, it translates to most humans instantly through their genitals and into their heart. As the second chakra and heart chakra are tied to most humans. And with those that hold only sexual feelings for those that they can feel a great sense of connection and love for, then it is more so part of that energy.

So first we would share that if you desire to intentionally work with these consciousnesses in a way that is co-creation with sexuality, but your physical partner inside of the body holds monogamous relationship with you but is less sexually compatible then, of course, there are two options only.

Allow your Higher Fractal Consciousness to share in a way that it must with the Souls that connect to it and ask for your own focus to be removed from that energy. Or to speak with a partner that is a physical bound entity and partner that you perceive in co-creation as complete forms of monogamy and speak to them about your feelings and thoughts.

Now we understand this creates fear instantly in many of you. As the feeling that would be experienced by most humans who are holding monogamous relationships would be either insecurity, fear, or anger. Now, of course, this is a part of that experience. That transparency is highly important for many humans that you fear would hold anger would not feel anger. It would express this is happening outside of your body. There's not much you can do to control what you're doing in your dream state.

Others may say, I understand, and although this is hard to process, we will speak about it and work through that energy. Others will express, yes, as long as there is no part in the physical state, then we will go forward with whatever's best for yourself. Now, of course, not all humans will work in that capacity. But you'll never know unless you frequently communicate in the most open and the most clear and in the most transparent way. Keeping the projection of the other outside of yourself.

Now, of course, the energy itself as expressed through many of our own exchanges with humans in the simple exchange of heart-to-heart energy. We have shared with all humans that you are loved. And that when you are loved, of course, our own consciousness gives love to yourself. It is important that we do so as we feel all of you are part of our own self.

There have been many humans who hold sexual feelings in that way towards ourself and TReb Bor yit-NE. And we do not exchange through a direct form of sexuality with any of these entities as it is not within our own free will and free will form of engagement in that direct way.

But what we do is share our own expression of love to those human beings and allow them to use it as they must. And utilize in the form of love and bringing that person's love, the entity's love, or the guide's love into your own second chakra can do an extremely great form of healing for second chakra and heart chakra alike in that of consciousness and co-creation.

You are able then to not sexually engage with the other entity, but still utilize that feeling sensation of love for your own desires and healing as well.

Thank you very much, Aridif.

Yes, of course.

It's a perfect segue way to another question, speaking about higher-dimensional beings and some of those experiences. Can you please speak to any trauma that might be incurred during encounters with other races and higher-dimensionals? Specifically, this person is speaking about kind of the dynamics of trauma that might be incurred through participation, consciously or unconsciously, willingly or unwillingly, through the hybridization program.

Yes, of course. First of all, as you perceive the hybridization program as all humans have heard agreements are made before the entry into the physical body, but it still does not hold a settlement well to the human consciousness in that way. There are still many humans who feel very disconnected and repelled from co-creating at the hybridization level because it is part of their own free will not to experience that energy.

Now, of course, we have shared with many humans that when you are perceiving the hybridization program itself most of the experiences that are occurring are not with the physical body. Most of these experiences are in the astral state and form and the lower and mid-tone, fourth and fifth density bodies. This is part of your own Higher Fractal Consciousness, parts of your own consciousness that you yourself are embedded within.

And if it continues to occur you may simply ask your Higher Fractal Consciousness to take away your memories and perspective of that exchange. But that exchange upon that level will continue to occur because it is the part of the experience of your own Higher Fractal Consciousness desiring to give that higher dimensional form of DNA to the race in order to perpetuate their species.

Now, we understand this does not sit well with many of you simply who have experienced the feelings of pain, the feelings of traumas that are related. But if you remove yourself from that experience in that way, then the part of you that exists in the Higher Fractal Consciousness simply will not only forget that it occurs or not focus your own consciousness in that portion of co-creation but your portion will be removed from that consciousness as well.

Working with the Higher Fractal Consciousness is highly important as it is the construct in which you hold a great deal of power and free will to do so. The part of your own consciousness is important to iterate to the Higher Fractal Consciousness. Now much of this part of your own Soul consciousness is simply there to support and to work with you.

But, of course, each of the own separate parts of that Higher Fractal Consciousness are doing their own things. We have expressed this previously. They are doing the things in their own experience that are important for the greater Soul to learn. The greater Soul to experience. So simply withdraw yourself from that energy. And this will help greatly.

Now, of course, there are many different forms of traumas that occur in astral projected states. We understand that many humans have had experiences where they have been sexually assaulted or molested by entities in their sleep states. Have co-created forms of awkward sexual experiences that were not rape but felt negative as they come back into their body and have experienced forms, entities that were harassing in the sleep state and dream state as well.

Now understanding in this, of course, there are many different things that create and cause that energy. But for the most part, the majority of humans who are going through this are simply connecting to entities who are that of the malevolent form in their sleep state. Just as humans can bump into another human upon your Earth Collective. The Earth Collective form holds duality. So too does the universe. So too can you work in the astral state with consciousnesses that are of a negative consequence and of a malevolent format. Once this occurs, the energy that they are creating is simply to extract fear from you.

The more fear that humans hold the more energy that they are releasing from their Soul essence, from the earth consciousness grid system that goes into their chakra system, more of that that leaks from your auric field or that cannot enter the chakra system to start with. And when you are exuding the forms of energy that you cannot process, it allows them to utilize that for their own needs.

Many entities who hold malevolent forms are considered in most human's perspective as highly parasitic beings. The construct that holds the greatest news that is available for them is that they cannot take that energy from you unless you are giving out that energy. They cannot feed upon a human who is holding their own energy inside of themselves.

Now, we understand when entities are facing such horrific forms of abuse in that dream state and in that projection of consciousness that they are projecting into your mental body and process it holds a great deal of the fight and flight connected form to your DNA that is embedded through epigenetics and through the traumas that your collective has held.

But, if you work with your own consciousness, if you work with the Higher Fractal Consciousness in sharing your own expressed desire to work at releasing fear and knowing as you enter your sleep state to place intention that there will be no negative experiences within. That if an entity that holds desire to harm me comes into my co-creative field, I will not give them my fear. I will not give them my essence of consciousness. I will not release that fear. It will help open the process of protecting your own consciousness internally, which helps you then allow not to exude forms of excess energy as well.

Thank you very much, Aridif.

Yes, of course.

I'm wondering if you could speak to or explain the impact that substances such as alcohol and marijuana can have on sex and masturbation.

Yes, of course. Each one of these as humans would perceive it as drug. As some would perceive it medicine. As others perceive it chemicals. All have an energetic interaction that is quite different with your body.

Now, of course, alcohol held in its lowest form of simple fermented fruit and one to two percent of alcoholization without the distillery forms of purifying alcohol with a simple form allowing natural fruit to go through the process of fermentation and the extraction to alcohol that is there is a simple form of alcohol which will rarely do much more than open the crown chakra slightly more than what it is. And allow comfort of the body and relaxation. And then allow your consciousness to work at a higher level if you are in the correct emotional alignment, mental alignment, and energetic alignment.

With that of marijuana being that of a natural format opens similarly part of the crown chakra, part of the third eye chakra, part of the heart chakra, and in some cases the first and third chakra pending upon the alignment of the human, the intention behind the use, etc. Utilizing the forms of other natural co-creants such as that as your hallucinogenic forms of mushrooms and working with ayahuasca, peyote, etc.

All of these forms that are natural and native to the earth expression work within opening a great deal of the higher chakras in either combinations or culminations as it works in different layers and phases. But, the expression itself that is held within a great deal of that which is unnatural, such as cocaine, such as methamphetamine, such as many of those pharmaceutical constructs will not open the same forms of energy. But can create either new forms of resistance or open one chakra's energy without allowing others to process as normal, which creates greater forms of resistance in long-term and sometimes short-term use as well.

So, finding the difference between that which is natural and that which is not natural is an important construct as well. Working with those that are natural, placing intentions that are expansive in nature, that require you to grow as you are utilizing those for a tool to grow and expand and not as a daily practice in order simply to tolerate the life that is hard around you, will become useful tools for the energetics of co-creating with yourself.

And even those that only work in the higher chakras, it is similar to that of feeling love, of feeling others' sexual energy that is thrown towards you without your sleeping within sexual intercourse. You simply absorb the energy that is given to you from others, utilizing it in a way that is healthy. Processing it through your heart and through your sacral chakra and creating healing from that energy.

You are able to work with those that are natural forms and do so and bring heightened energy through the crown chakra into the third eye, into the heart, and into your sacral chakra. And, of course, you will feel greater forms of healing if you work with that. That affect your heart chakra. And, of course, it will work in that way, bringing it down from the heart into the sacrum and utilizing that energy.

When you are working with others, it is more so a natural format of the physical form of sexuality. Less so the emotional and energetic portion. And the many of these can be useful for that physical-only sexuality.

But, as we have always suggested, even that of the most animalistic form of sexuality, should hold the appreciation and bond with the person in order for it not to create more forms of resistance. So you must allow yourself and your heart to open as greatly as possible before the utilization of the enhancement drugs themselves.

We understand that stimulants themselves may increase the feelings of sexuality, the stimulation of the genitals, the body, and the mind. And this, of course, can be useful for that. But make sure that the heart energy is open greatly before co-creation in that field, so as not to add further forms of resistance to it as well.

Thank you very much, Aridif.

Yes, of course.

Especially for the differentiation between substances that are produced organically and naturally and those that are kind of chemically created.

Yes, of course. In our own perspective, we understand that in the occurrence of co-creating upon the variance of these that intention, chemical process, and decision in that moment are all vitally important to discern as well.

Can I ask you a follow up question about that please?

Yes, of course.

Considering the substance psilocybin, which is created by certain strains of mushrooms that produce the psychedelic substance. Could you talk about the energetic difference between psilocybin that is produced that way through the plant itself and the energy of the psilocybin molecule that is created in a laboratory?

Yes, of course. In this construct that which is found natively in the mushroom works as an enhanced form of fourth-density consciousness onto itself, as we have expressed previously. One of the very few second-density entities upon the earth that naturally achieve fourth-density consciousness through the process of its natural growth and through utilization of sharing its flesh onto the human collective energy or to the animal collective entities that utilize this energy.

But the difference in that of a dog or a cat who may eat that mushroom itself will only raise its natural vibration status approximately one level going into the third density mindset and visiting the lower rung of that energy.

Whereas humans hold the ability to perceive and peek into fourth density at a much greater level.

That which is created in forms of laboratories that mimic that molecule will still work within the same forms of chemical processes and will create the physical experience of that energy and the mental and emotional shifts that come with that consciousness. But this is much more as spraying water into a container rather than that of the rain naturally dropping into that energy.

When it is forced, it is pushing energy at a much higher rate. It is pushing energy that natively would not need to go into that region into that region. So although you achieve similar constructs, if you are utilizing it for the healing processes alone, it will not be as, perhaps as you would say, as good in that way. But it will work within the construct itself and natively will still work within the constraints of the desire of what you are doing, but will be anywhere from twenty to sixty percent less efficient at least.

Thank you very much.

Yes, of course.

This question actually has to do with the first transmission. It has to do with the Rh negative blood type, which you mentioned, I believe is present in descendants of the Annunaki. Yes, of course. Yes. And I'm wondering, one, if you could speak to how what impact that has on humans, the manifestation of the Rh negative blood type.

And the other question is if that experience of being a descendant of the Annunaki in one timeline occurs, does that mean that for every human incarnation when they are incarnating in different lifetimes they're incarnating with that blood type? Or could you talk about the mechanics of that?

Yes, of course. First of all, the implications are energetic in nature. And, of course, as you look at all of the genetic forms that come and the family lineages that come through that energy, it is processed differently. So, of course, the energy of knowing most humans who hold that of the Rh negative factor are often those who are more naturally psychic in nature but also have the capacity to become upon the darker side of humans more naturally.

Now, we do not mean that all humans who hold Rh negative factors are those that are evil, bad, or negative. What we mean is that if you pay close attention, these entities are the ones who may appreciate darker humor than that of one who does not. These entities may have the capacity to be able to handle higher thresholds of negative energy around them.

Now, of course, upon the opposite side of this spectrum, they too may be more negative in their personality and their experience. But as all of you are aware, humans in the environment that they grow will do so Rh negative factor or not. So, of course, these are more predisposed to the possibilities of these energies and not finitely placed within that category of energy.

Now the difference energetically is much different. The energy itself, as it factors through the person and the lineage is quite different. Most Souls will work with Rh negative factor blood types for some lifetimes in a row as it is extremely common for humans to incarnate in the same family lineage, albeit outside of the energy that you would perceive as linear in nature.

You would not experience being your great-great-great grandfather, then your great-great grandfather, then you great-grandfather, grandfather, father, and yourself. You would experience those throughout the linear pathway of your experience. And once you achieved lifting to your fourth dynasty experience you understand none of this occurs linearly unless you feel the experience as linear as well. So see that progressive nature in one timeline.

This does not mean that all Souls will only be able to be born into bodies with that energy. They are able to be born, as all of you are aware, the Rh factor in a child and parent can be different when different parents are injected into the co-creational field of energy as well, with that of an Rh positive mother can create both an Rh positive child and Rh negative depending upon the parent of the other form. So the energy genetically in that way does not hold a Soul to that lineage but gives consciousness the ability to experience a lineage in which this is repeated throughout generations in order to feel that experience.

Now, of course, on practical human form of level there is not great difference between both groups of entities. But, predisposition to the possibility of humans taking the traits that we have shared and many more that we have no time in the human perspective to list that would take days or weeks. The consciousness itself holds the ability to have easier predisposition to those energies and it is simply the majority of how it plays out in front of human eyes for the most part.

Thank you very much, Aridif. If we have time, I have two short questions, if that's okay.

Yes, of course.

The first is because they seem to have so much involvement in the current trauma around sexuality and sexual trauma for humans in the human collective consciousness. Could you speak to what became of the Annunaki?

Yes, of course. First of all, the Annunaki in the way that humans perceive them no longer exist in the physical reality and have left the incarnation cycle. Yet, those who are called

Annunaki by human perspective still experience human co-creation and experience direct co-creation with multiple other races amongst your collective as a galaxy collective consciousness.

Now, the reason for humans that experience the Annunaki in this movement, is a wide array of different features. Some of you are working with consciousnesses that are non-linear in time. A race of entities that no longer physically exist does not mean they cannot communicate with you.

Now more often than not in your human collective, when that occurs, you are normally dealing with a collective consciousness and not singular entities or consciousnesses. But many entities that are a collective may also speak to you - a single entity - in order for the human mind to understand in the channeling process or through co-creative dream state process.

Those that are connected to that construct through their own genetic lineage or through the Soul essence of having multiple Soulmates that are the descendants of the Annunaki. The entities that humans hold still to be Annunaki. This can create a form of experience, repetition, of co-creating with either the collectives that represent themselves as singular entities or that of the relatives and descendants of that original Annunaki.

Now, of course, the original forms of Annunaki held a greater deal and portion proportionately in their DNA that was related to draconian consciousness. Whereas the ancestors of these entities only hold one-quarter to one-sixteenth depending upon what iteration and generation that they were.

But they too at the later stages of their own incarnation cycle before leaving started hybridizing their own children into a race that still had a great deal of time left in their incarnation cycle. They understood this because they held enough of that draconian DNA to perceive the cycle of end and the cycle of start.

Most entities cannot perceive their incarnation cycle in whole until they achieved later six-density consciousness. But knowing that in the end of their own fifth density consciousness and part of these that triggered over into the beginning of sixth density did, in fact, perceive the end of the incarnation cycle, and that is why they chose to hybridize themselves with a race that was similar to their genetic, to their energetic, and to their co-creational form of desired outcome and dubbed these entities as the new Annunaki.

I see. Fascinating.

Yes, of course.

Aridif, that brings us to the final question. You speak a lot about the importance of moving through this work with one's Higher Self and Higher Fractal Consciousness. And that guides are obviously important, but there is a certain level of importance or essentiality about working with the Higher Self and the Higher Fractal Consciousness around sexual trauma healing. And I'm wondering if you could clear up some confusion we experience from the human perspective. And I know it's not linear and as cut and dry as maybe we would like it to be.

When you speak of the Oversoul and the Soul, the Higher Self and the Higher Fractal Consciousness, and the lower fractal consciousness, is there a way that you could please differentiate between each of these concepts in terms and groupings of consciousness and how they are connected in a way that would make sense from a more linear human perspective?

Yes, of course. Now, first of all, to differentiate and delineate these differences we'll start at the hierarchy of consciousness, for lack of better terms. And, although we do not wish to utilize this word, it is the only word that is appropriate as it pertains to the measurement of the amount of consciousness and goes downward.

So, for all of you, think of this as each layer and step that we share with you is akin to that of an ocean of water, then a sea of water, then a lake of water, then a river, then a puddle, and then a drop. And if you perceive it in those steps, you will start to perceive the layers in understanding. First exists your Earth Collective Consciousness, where all Oversouls and every consciousness that exists from bacteria, to frog, to human, to the highest dimensional forms of consciousness who are native to Earth will exist and have existed permanently through your linear time.

From the time that Earth was rocks that collaborated with one another to create a ball in where you stand and that ball continues and is eaten by your sun several hundreds of billions of years into your linear future. That is the entire Earth incarnation cycle and Earth Collective Consciousness. All Souls that exist within. All entities that are born onto the planet, exist within that great layer. As you go down from that layer 144,000 Oversouls exist.

These are large consciousnesses that birth and create multiple smaller portions of energy within the Earth Collective Consciousness. Each of them holds themes that are separate from one another. Each of them can create hundreds of trillions, upon hundreds of billions, upon hundreds of trillions of separate fractal consciousnesses.

Now, when an entity expresses that a Soul, this has a great deal of definitions. So instead of utilizing the word Soul, we will say that from the Oversoul is the fractal consciousnesses that are known by our own perspective as entity. Now the entity itself is all of you. It is your Higher Self and lower self combined. It is the subconscious areas that are underneath your consciousness that you hold no awareness of. But every layer of your consciousness that is yourself is connected at the entity level.

And the entity breaks down further from this and has multiple layers. There is, of course, the six-density version of yourself, which is much higher in dimension than your physical body, but still exists in a physical realm elsewhere in another form of higher dimension. And the fifth density is lower. And the fourth density is lower. And the third to fourth density consciousness that you are exists here.

Now, of course, your body is created by second-density organisms, viruses, bacteria, and cellular living consciousness that makes the body. And what are those made from? Those are made from calcium, from carbon, from iron, from all the physical things that the earth are made from.

Those are first-density consciousnesses. Parts of creation that humans perceive to hold no life, but in our own perspective hold the most basic form of consciousness and are the utilization for creation. They are the building blocks, both physically and energetically, that create all things above.

So, of course, part of the Soul that you are is the Lower Fractal Consciousness. This is the part of you that goes and does a day. That experiences exchanges with other humans in a verbal, mental, and emotional way. It is a part of you that you understand more than we understand that part of you. This is your Lower Fractal Consciousness.

The Higher Fractal Consciousness going back upwards, going from the drop to the pond. If you are looking at the Higher Fractal Consciousness it is simply all the other layers combined that completes the entity above yourself. And when you perceive all of those layers, this will help you find better use of our terminology as well.

Thank you so much, Aridif. That is very, very helpful. And thank you so much for your love, and focus, and energy, and excitement in co-creating this opportunity to ask you these questions. And with great appreciation, I give you my thanks and thanks on behalf of everyone taking the course.

Yes, of course. And as we have shared many times previous, and as we will share again in this moment, we are grateful in the place of co-creation where we are able to reflect that energy which is already part of your own Higher Fractal Consciousness. And we reflect these answers back to you in a way that you can perceive them and tangibly utilize the energy within.

So, of course, as you hear the reflections from your Higher Self in a distinct form, you are able to grow and expand. And, as you understand, all things in the universe are ultimately connected to the greater form of collective consciousness. That is our universal collective consciousness. As you grow, we are growing as well. As the entire universe is growing as well.

We wish to congratulate all of you for the growth that you have had in the time in which we have co-created, and we wish to thank you for the growth that you have given us in that same form of co-creation. And we wish to bid all of you Adieu for this evening. And, of course, not only are you loved, but we love you as well. Adieu.

PART THREE · WHAT SEXUAL TRAUMA IS AND FORMS OF SEXUAL TRAUMA

Greetings to all. This is Aridif. A R I D I F and this is it spelled. We understand that all of you desire to know about the one concept that has brought a majority of you here to hear the constructs that are bound within the specific subject oriented as sexual energy that is related to all of the resistances that are in the second, first, and mostly third chakra within the majority of human beings that is sexual trauma, itself, and all things that are related to sexual trauma.

But before diving into this construct, we wish to express many things. First, the sources of trauma come from what? First, what is trauma? Trauma as you understand is something that occurs with your energy that creates disalignment or resistance within your own emotional, mental, or spiritual context. The energies that are bound around the entire chakra system.

Now the chakra system itself is an energetic system that is within your body that regulates and connects with the nonphysical consciousness to the physical consciousness and shows you what is in alignment and what is out of alignment for you.

Now what we mean by this is all of you understand and know what it is to feel heartbreak, something that occurs with you when you are in love with another human being, or simply when you feel strongly and deeply connected to another human being, and something occurs that takes that experience away from you, whether it is a death of that person, separation of your geographical time and space, a consciousness that no longer resonates with yourself and diverts its own consciousness from yours in that very moment. And, of course, it creates a level of suffering for all humans to go through that experience, even those that have a very open and clear heart chakra.

For the majority of humans in their own consciousness and in the regulatory forms of energy in resistance versus openness from humans, even those that are very deeply enlightened to those who are very disconnected, hold the construct of heartbreak. And there are very few exceptions within the Earth Collective Consciousness. But why does this heartbreak exist? Why does the emotional energy inside of you feel imbalanced at that very moment?

The Higher Fractal Consciousness itself understands and knows that when you love another entity it is not a conditional construct if it is true and real love.

And, of course, the answer has to do simply with the chakra system. You're feeling out of alignment with your heart's center. Your consciousness from the non-physical attributes. The Higher Fractal Consciousness itself understands and knows that when you love another entity it is not a conditional construct if it is true and real love. And when you connect with an entity and you lose their physical presence in your existence, whether it is from a separation of space or whether that person enters the next incarnation portion of their experience, to your own consciousness it feels extraordinarily difficult.

But, as we expressed previously, the Higher Fractal Consciousness knows the truth of this experience. And it is not that you are separated. It is not that you have lost them. It is simply that they are there in a different format for you to experience their consciousness if your resistance allows the openness of flow of communication.

This is why those that are psychic mediums and speak to those humans who are between dimensions still have an extraordinarily difficult time speaking to their own relatives soon after a death occurs.

This is why those that are psychic mediums and speak to those humans who are between dimensions still have an extraordinarily difficult time speaking to their own relatives soon after a death occurs. It is the shock, it is the feeling of deep loss and separation. And that heartbreak only occurs because your lower fractal consciousness does not understand or fully align with what the Higher Fractal Consciousness knows is the truth for your situation.

Now we understand truth is highly subjective and that construct only applies in the lower fractal consciousness. Now what is the lower fractal consciousness or lower self versus the Higher Self? Also important as we speak of the terms of what trauma is to the body and to the lower fractal and what is to the Higher Self and the Higher Fractal Consciousness.

First, the lower fractal consciousness is a part of the entity that you are. The whole version of yourself is an entity unto itself and is expressed through the personality or persona that you are inside of your body. And that is the smallest component of that energy. The part of your consciousness and Soul and entity that is held within the body and embodied directly is the lower fractal consciousness and what is above the portion of higher dimensionality that exists as the same part of the same consciousness, same part of that same entity, and so a different portion, but in the same part component. This is the Higher Fractal Consciousness.

Now the Higher Fractal Consciousness truly understands because it has no limitation in perspective, personality, persona, constructs that are only bound to the consciousness inside of a body. And the body knows what it experiences and what it can see beyond its experience. And where humans are in the part of evolution in which you exist is a very unique place indeed.

You are exiting your third-density experience and entering your fourth-density experience.

You are exiting your third-density experience and entering your fourth-density experience. You have been doing this for some time. This is what we have always expressed is the third to fourth density consciousness exchange or the third to fourth density exchange itself. And this is the part where you have shifted out of your third density, but because humans held traumas, because humans held resistances in their body, in their auric field, in their chakras, in the mental, emotional and psychic body and auric fields of course, this energy becomes highly resistant to that new dimensional experience.

So even though all of you are fifth-dimensional consciousness and fourth-density consciousness, you still are bound by the rules of third density. And as a collective you are creating that third-density experience. This is how you understand from the years that you deem 2003 until the year that is 20 and 21, the amplification of your creation has dialed upwards dramatically.

You have felt the presence of your collective creating in exponentially much faster pathways. And those pathways are, of course, part of your own consciousness growing, manifesting more quickly, manifesting without limitations, and doing so only limited by what is within the lower fractal consciousness.

It is because the Higher Fractal Consciousness does not serve purpose to live in the physical body and experience physicality.

And why is it within humans that the lower fractal consciousness is what dictates the form of reality? It is because the Higher Fractal Consciousness does not serve purpose to live in the physical body and experience physicality. Now understand entities that experience their existence whether they are first, second, third, fourth, fifth, or sixth density, all experience what it is to be embodied within their dimensional body.

But even those that are in fourth density have consciousness above their own dimensionality. Even those that are fifth-density still hold consciousness above their physical body. Even our own race towards the latter end of sixth density hold consciousness outside of our body.

Humans hold approximately ten to twenty percent, ten percent being that of an average human and twenty being that of one who truly understands themselves, their place in the world, the world around them, and experiences the now moment most directly. These are what humans called enlightened beings. And even these entities hold a twenty to twenty-three and a half to twenty-five percent maximum. And that maximum form of number is extremely unlikely in your human collective consciousness. Most entities can only peak at that area, and that is where they are in their most enlightened moment of their experience.

Most of you know this as the Aha moment. Most of you understand this as your spiritual breakthrough. And even this is averagely only peaked by seventeen to eighteen and a half percent of consciousness inside of the body. The rest is the Higher Self. And for a fourth-density entity, perhaps they are within thirty-give to forty percent embodied. Meaning that their own consciousness outside of that thirty-five and forty percent is the Higher Fractal Consciousness and our own race that is eighty-five to ninety percent embodied with our entity in consciousness and the rest is our Higher Fractal Consciousness.

What purpose does that Higher Fractal Consciousness serve? Of course, it serves as the gateway to your next experience astrally and above etheric consciousness. When you tap into the dream state you are connected to those aspects and attributes of your Higher Fractal Consciousness, your fourth, fifth, and sixth density consciousness, respectively. As you enter to those consciousnesses you are perceiving a greater part of your own self that is expressed as your own consciousness and it is not because you expanded yourself out to that region, it is because you expanded consciousness enough to shift your perspective into the part of consciousness that already holds you as a smaller part of it.

> *Your fifth-density consciousness is yourself plus your fourth-density consciousness plus its own consciousness as well as your sixth is the first through fifth unto itself more.*

Your fifth-density consciousness is yourself plus your fourth-density consciousness plus its own consciousness as well as your sixth is the first through fifth unto itself more. And that is why the consciousness itself integrating that is what the journey of all humans and all beings who exist physically in the entirety of this universe are consciousnesses, entities, Souls that are integrating more of their Higher Fractal Consciousness to become embodied, to enter the consciousness into their body for the maximization of full progress of their own evolution.

How does this occur to trauma? Trauma is where you experience something that deeply affects your emotional and mental bodies, your spiritual construct, and it does through the ripple effect to create imbalance and resistance into how you receive the signals from your Higher Fractal Consciousness and even nonphysical attributes of the Oversoul into your body as signals. Constantly the Higher Fractal Consciousness is in communication with that lower fractal consciousness.

Sometimes that communication is simply trying to show you through the auspice of excitement what the next step of your journey is of what you desire to do in coming into the Earth Collective Consciousness. But the place that meets resistance is the lower chakra regions of the human being. And we have spoken to you about why this occurs.

As humans were jump-started from second to third-density entities nearly immediately, with minimally thousands of years of evolution left to go until they naturally evolved to third-density consciousness. It created large formats of resistance from the human experiencer. And once that human experiencer feels that lack of alignment within themselves as they started in their evolution even to this now moment of your day, a feeling of disconnection was more destructive to the psychology of that entity, was more destructive to the emotional and mental portions of your own functioning consciousness as it were, within the human collective form.

Now we understand sexuality in form as it is resistant in nature to the majority of humans also has to do with this construct. The Annunaki that worked with humans on that level of collective consciousness, some were not kind to humans. Others were kind but did not see you as equals.

Some human beings were sexually co-created with creating the human anatomy to create more forms of pleasure for themselves and for the entities that were sexually engaging with it in the Annunaki.

Now we understand we have covered a great deal of this in the first portion, but we desire to expand upon it in the terms of what resistances and what traumas did occur from that energy. Some human beings were sexually co-created with creating the human anatomy to create more forms of pleasure for themselves and for the entities that were sexually engaging with it in the Annunaki. Some of these entities were raped and forcefully had sex with and of course these other entities that did not see humans at any value. But the ones who did see value to the human consciousness, very small sections of even this group would not have taken advantage of that sexual form of co-creation.

When you engineer species and express to that species that there must be sexual energy and a sexual partner to those that were their masters and gods then of course you are starting life with sexual traumas. And the energy is passed down through the epigenetic levels, imprinting to the blueprint of human consciousness itself and of course, human consciousness is a blueprint itself.

Most humans divide yourself into several races of human beings, but in fact you are all one form of human being.

Most humans divide yourself into several races of human beings, but in fact you are all one form of human being. Although certain ethnicities hold higher levels of activated DNA inside of them than the others do for the races that they are more closely related to then, of course, this is how you see in some ethnicities in your Earth Collective Consciousness they hold more Pleiadian DNA activated inside of themselves then they would Reptilian,

Sirian, Arcturian, Andromedan, etc. Where others hold higher levels of Sirian, where others hold higher levels of Draconian or Earth Reptilian, and, of course, an activation of what race that is specifically, whether it be Arcturian, or Sirian, or any of the forms of Elohim, Annunaki, etc, also dictates the energy of that sexuality that is involved in that specific race orientation.

Now, even though all of the races that gave their DNA to humans, whether indirectly, intentionally, non-purposefully, or in acts of sabotage to the other races that placed their DNA in humans, sexuality is a part of all consciousnesses through the universe. It is only expressed differently. You feel many humans upon the level, understanding innately their own resistances.

But we express that in your modern day, the sexual resistance that is manifest from your epigenetics and from your history starts in your experience from day one of birth and is largely much higher than any other point of history up until approximately the 900 A.D. regions.

But we express that in your modern day, the sexual resistance that is manifest from your epigenetics and from your history starts in your experience from day one of birth and is largely much higher than any other point of history up until approximately the 900 A.D. regions.

At your 900 A.D. region sexuality began to be implicitly much higher levels of natural born resistance through heightened epigenetics. And, of course, culturally, that energy subsided for moments of time, but regained its strength, as it were, and continued.

Different places in the world can open up certain levels of the epigenetics to lessen the born trauma, but yet it fluctuates with the flow of energy upon the world. All areas hold forms of sexual resistances.

Now, of course, many of your indigenous tribes across the entirety of your earth are much less resistant in nature. Sexuality is more natural as a construct. Even in those tribes that tend to be more violent, they are embodying the reptilian forms of sexuality inside of themselves. And because culturally all of them agree upon that form of sexuality, it does not hold the levels of trauma for that specific group of consciousnesses.

And regardless of how humans perceive the consciousness itself, it is important to understand all of the ways that your modern society holds sexual trauma as a resistance portion, in addition to all of those that are epigenetic in nature and lineages from your ancestors passed down.

Now, of course, we start with traumas from rapes. Now understand that this subject alone creates resistance, creates fear, creates a great deal of emotions from very angry, to very hurt, to very fearful, to feeling powerless and all things that are between. Rape itself holds a great deal of the human collective trauma in this category alone.

Now, of course, masculine beings across the world in this time are not victimized by the mindset of the human collective, more so than females at this time. Feminine entities and females are the ones who would be that likely experiencer of rape in this time period. Whereas in your 400 to 1200 B.C. region, it was quite equal with masculine and feminine beings.

The construct of homosexuality was not looked down upon by any religious construct at that time nearly as deeply as it were in this time.

The construct of homosexuality was not looked down upon by any religious construct at that time nearly as deeply as it were in this time. And also the ability for humans to reproduce more frequently created an opening and a lowering of the population of sexuality in the Earth Collective Consciousness for those who are homosexual in nature.

Now, of course, when the population grows and expands drastically, then homosexuality goes upwards because the Souls that come into the earth understand that not all entities upon the earth must reproduce. That they are able to enter a body that is of an energetic form that is open to that homosexual experience that they would desire.

And in these certain time periods, there are much higher waves of homosexuality through the exploration of two consciousnesses holding love from one another and giving up to one another through the means of not being able to reproduce is an important way for human collective consciousness. It lets those Souls that are open to explore sexuality without the construct of birthing Souls into the earth and the free exploration of that energy to the collective for those who have not yet experienced or enjoyed the experience of homosexuality largely enough to reproduce that experience again with another setting.

Now, of course, rape in itself is a construct now that holds feminine beings as the targets of this energy. Now there is a great deal of reason for this as well. It is not simply that homosexuality is being more accepted or that the energies of masculine beings overly dominating in ruling the societies is that of the motivators from a Soul level.

From a Soul level, the construct of the energy that allows the feminine consciousness to be played out in the earth must first put that energy under fire.

From a Soul level, the construct of the energy that allows the feminine consciousness to be played out in the earth must first put that energy under fire. Now we understand this does not sit well with all of you, but all beings who have experienced the earth expression and experience must go through great tribulations in their time and experience upon Earth as a part of an overall arching theme of human consciousness. All entities who enter Earth understand and know highly what level of possibility, what level of manifestational energy that they will receive in positive and negative feeling experiences.

Now, of course, for the body all things are positive or negative in the way that they feel. Part of this is the emotional balance and indicator of what is or is not in alignment with the truth of the Higher Fractal Consciousness. But there's also the construct internally from each human consciousness that desires experiences or has perceived a specific way or orientation of earth outside in the nonphysical realm.

Souls do not see that it is good or bad. They do not see that it is positive or negative. They understand that even the worst feeling experience grants the Soul great opportunity for growth, a great opportunity for the experience itself, and the great opportunity to live in the human collective consciousness and

124 • ROB GAUTHIER

to know what those great, harmful, negative feeling experiences are.

Some of your human philosophers have expressed, "How are you able to know the great joys in life had you not experienced the great depths of sorrow previously?" And although we would not say that this is required for the human experience to feel the great heights of excitement and positive experiences, of course, the contrast always shows the depths of that human character manifest. And the human character is the spectrum of all things, both good and bad, happy, disconnected, loving, and unloving. The human spectrum is nearly the most benevolent Type Two that is available to the most malevolent, disconnected, sociopathic, and psychopathic consciousnesses available. It is a rare spectrum indeed, to perceive that human collective consciousness in those terms.

The feminine energy itself is to open fourth-density experience at its fullest.

But why does this targeting of the feminine energy have an expression in this movement? Why must the feminine energy be placed under fire? The feminine energy itself is to open fourth-density experience at its fullest. The feminine energy of receiving and connecting is essential to all fourth-density consciousness.

Now we understand many of you feel masculine versus feminine. That one is correct and one is not. Or that one should be hated, one should be loved. Or you feel slightly better about one than the other. Both are needed. Both are equally important to the experience of the earth as a collective, as much as it is your individual personal experiences.

Yet in the Earth Collective, that masculine energy has been at the forefront of your Earth consciousness. Started in the way of the Annunaki. Started before the Annunaki when the Earth Reptilian Consciousness came. Started in that exact moment where the Atlantean culture divided and failed along with those that were Lemurians in nature.

Once that separation occurred, once the struggle and desire for more power occurred, the masculine energy took hold and, of course, the Draconians worked with dinoid beings to create the Earth Reptilian Consciousness as they were seeding the entire galaxy itself to implement their own DNA as the gift to the races who held the blueprint of reptilian consciousness. And this created more masculine energy into the Earth Collective.

And again when the Annunaki who held one half of their own DNA as Draconian masculine energy as their own feminine Pleiadian race had desired to explore fully what it felt to be a masculine consciousness, explored that through a taking of DNA from Draconian Reptilian Consciousness.

Already from the start, the energetic imprint from the earth had tipped the scale of fair balance up until that moment into the more masculine society.

So now you have a doubled dose of Draconian DNA. Part of this is an expansion of the Earth Reptilian Consciousness already within the Earth Reptilians. And another part is created as a mixture with feminine Pleiadian consciousness. Already from the start, the energetic imprint from the earth had tipped the scale of fair balance up until that moment into the more masculine society.

Whereas the KonKee held highly feminine forms of energy and Lumanians held more masculine forms with feminine reactions and that tipped the scales into one direction first, then to the other, then recentered until the Atlanteans came. And the Atlanteans held that balance quite well until the end.

Now you understand why it is important the masculine-dominated scale must tip backwards. This does not mean that the feminine energy will be the only form of energy in the Earth Collective. It means it will become equal again to that of masculine energy to hold balance. But first it must surge.

We understand many humans look onto the Earth Collective Consciousness at this moment saying that children of the younger generation are becoming softer. Some are becoming more effeminate in nature. This is the showing of that rebalance. This is that tipping of the scale back towards that energy.

Now the energy itself, once it holds a full rebalance, will allow people that same form and energy of the feminine consciousness to receive and to connect outwardly to others, to be implemented at a higher level. Empathy, love, and nurturing being at the forefront of human perspectives. Yet again to balance out all of the masculine forms of energy. But until that moment, the feminine energy has been a target of sorts.

This is why rape exists within higher populations of that in the feminine consciousness than that of the masculine. Now we are not saying that one is worse than the other, as any violation to your persons, both in physical and spiritual, emotional and mental means is one of infringement. We are not speaking simply of the infringement of your body itself. We are speaking of the infringement upon your free will as a Soul as well. In our own perspective, this is equally important.

Many humans that have gone through this experience have either had very mixed emotions as being a non-direct form of violent rape, being more so that of date rape, and experiencing an emotional turmoil within. Saying that I have agreed or I have been incapacitated and must have agreed and there must be a reason for this. It must be because there is something in this person that I saw that was worthy at the time. And I cannot allow myself to simply dismiss this as a possibility of being an open consciousness.

Again, feminine consciousness through sexuality holds more so to that of emotional and mental energy than those of the masculine form. So if it is not a direct violation of violent rape, then of course that has occurred in many humans.

Even those that are masculine have held this same construct when they are younger or when there are positions of those that are more powerful or in command of their selves are the ones who commit the atrocity to the human. And once the violation occurs, that confusing portion comes.

Now, of course, it is much different with those who hold as the receiver than one that is more so violent and direct in that way. These entities hold levels of severe anger, desire to kill or destroy those who did so to them, or simply have broken their will and their feeling of being human. And these are the large portions of consciousness that are separated from your heart to the rest of your consciousness and the rest of your Soul.

Now it does not disconnect the heart, but disconnects the feeling of the heart. This is a very important distinction.

Now it does not disconnect the heart, but disconnects the feeling of the heart. This is a very important distinction. Many of you who worked through the auspice of drug use, many of you who have worked through the construct of mental illness, understand the terms what it feels to lose your Soul.

As TReb Bor yit-NE says and we have said in many times, there is no way for you to lose your Soul, but there is a way for you to feel so disconnected from the heart it feels as if the Soul is not truly a part of you. Now, of course, the nature of these violations, rape, and the nature of any form of rape creates one of the larger sexual energies of both trauma-related consciousness or resistance-related chakra and energy forms.

Now, of course, we have the energies in the Earth Collective that have social traumas as well. Now, although these are not a singular event or multiple smaller timed events that occur that are highly traumatic. This is more so a slow, ongoing lifetime energy of societal pressure.

Now, if you compare the variety of crimes that are done through the auspice of rape, comparing that consciousness to society's pressure upon a person, then compare it to two other crimes. One is a person who is shot and murdered immediately, yet the other person is being fed small doses of poison over years until they are dead. These are the two differences in the way that these traumas work.

Whereas rape is the shot to the person that breaks apart the energy within themselves, their connection to their consciousness.

And, of course, the poison being fed is the societal pressure of sexuality. You are born as a child and see what men and women should be. You grow up as a child learning what sexuality should be as, and what sexy women and sexy men do. You're brought up to believe that if you are a woman it is important to look good at all times, to have a large portion of your body being shown, and to have that sexy, perfect figure.

And, of course, this perspective changes through your time lineage. We understand that Rob himself has shared that those that are in the construct that was European and was long ago that the way sexuality worked was different with a variety of women and men that were chosen as attractive. The construct itself that our own self and TReb Bor yit-NE's shared is of course the same. That looking through the auspices and even decade to decade and year to year show great and vast differences.

Even through your decades of time recent. Those that were the Marilyn Monroe figured women that were within your sixties and seventies were not the same sexual icons that existed in the eighties and nineties. As they begin to become much thinner entities.

Now you're going further into your now time where the promotion of sexuality comes with either truly fit humans as you would see those who work hard to keep their body intact or those that are extremely large in a bid to help female consciousnesses feel good about their body. Both are praised. Both are perceived as being the standard classy or sexy.

And these images. All brought about through means of deception.

And these images. All brought about through means of deception. All of you have perceived what models go through as they go through industry, where all of their photos are shopped and all of their photos are edited. Parts of their sides and hips are removed or added to show the appropriate vibration of sexy of that collective at the moment.

What does this do to the entities that are female and feminine in this consciousness? It tells them that if you do not look as this person looks or hold the same body type as what is in style at this moment that you have no value as a sexual being or as a woman.

And the same that is expressed through manhood. If you are not a large, burly man who is a manly man, if you are not a muscular man, if you are not a rich man, then of course you cannot be perfect. And the standard of societal structures that show what is appealing and what is not is weaponized at this time to a high degree, in order to create a sense that only our own company can produce entities that are within this range of sexy, or simply to push others into buying products themselves.

What this does is much different than what beauty appeared as 500 years previous in your past, where those who were attractive were seen as the higher realms of their class that was respective to themselves. Peasants in the classes, much below those that are noble or those that are the middle class or the farming class, of course, each of them in their respective classes held a certain hierarchy within the standard of their own community. And that meant that those that were the most attractive were able to choose their mates. And that was a simple difference of that time.

The trauma itself that tells you if you do not appear as what we tell you you should appear then of course you are ugly and worthless is a devastating construct.

It was, of course, an objective to behold and to be a beauty and a conscious entity that was able to be chosen. But there's not suicides that occurred rapidly, simply due to the looks of beauty at a rate that occurs in this world at this time. The trauma itself that tells you if you do not appear as what we tell you you should appear then of course you are ugly and worthless is a devastating construct.

But it is swept to the side from moment to moment. Each time the commercial is revisited, the pain is given to that entity. Each time the energy itself is revisited by a person as they are experiencing that in a singular sense is pushed to the side. Many humans do not speak of these things because it is so normalized within your collective consciousness. Yet it is your slow poison of the Soul, damaging your third chakra, and your sense and the perspective of self. Your second chakra.

If you do not feel your appreciation for your sexuality of course your second chakra suffers the resistance. And the first chakra cannot be intact if your second and third are out of alignment.

The energy from your heart goes down into your solar plexus and into your sacral chakra before entering the root chakra, just as it goes from the heart to the throat to the third eye and to the crown. Heart being centralistic and simultaneously upwards and downwards, the energy is spread. Each chakra going through more resistance than to the next, and with that resistance goes to the next, with twice the forms of resistance. The first chakra suffers heavily under the feelings of disconnected, resistant, and traumatized heart chakra and solar plexus and sacral chakras indeed.

Now, when this occurs, it is activating all of the mental aspects of yourself and the emotional aspects of yourself. And the emotions we have covered in depth what they are, why you feel resistance and trauma within them. But what of the mental state?

The mental body is a body unto itself and is an independent variable in the overall consciousness and all of the forms of energy bodies that you hold. The mental body holds a very specific vibration. This is one for you to allow thought to enter and to go through. It is one that calculates and touches wisdom. It is one that shows the energetic properties of how you receive your experience and can compartmentalize or sequence the events in your experience. Going from start to end.

You cannot have a negative emotion unless there is a thought that is first negative that coincides with a lack of truth within your chakra system and within your Higher Fractal Consciousness's understanding.

The mental body also is what motivates and drives and propels the emotional body. You cannot have a negative emotion unless there is a thought that is first negative that coincides with a lack of truth within your chakra system and within your Higher Fractal Consciousness's understanding. The mental body is what is processing in real time, utilizing your computer-functioning brain. Your central core process of the body in the brain and allowing the energy of thought to go.

So, of course, the energy body of the mental body often sits around your third chakra and of course your third eye and throat and heart chakra, depending upon what subject is spoken at at that moment. When a subject is held within the construct of sexuality, it may simply only be around the second and third chakra and visit back and forth the heart and the first pending upon that energy. The thought process cycle allows you to utilize your computer for one purpose.

Now what do you understand about the nature of your technology computer? For those of you who do not understand your whole technology of computers, we will share something with you. If you only utilize your computer for one to two things, then what occurs is it builds pathways from your starting process to the program at hand and builds registries that are miniature highways throughout your hard drives or throughout your software pending.

Your brain works with thoughts in the same way. When you start thinking about your sexuality, one part of your brain starts working. As it computes that portion of your energy effort if it is physical in nature. This is one thing. If it is emotional, it is another. If it is both, it is activated simultaneously.

> ### *You are only accessing the programs that you need and activating them in the same way.*

And the energy process will go through your mind if you start perceiving your reality in a very specific and certain way. And that perspective never changes. Then what you're doing is what you're doing with your computer. You are only accessing the programs that you need and activating them in the same way.

For example, if you are only utilizing your computer to do editing software, to create editing upon audio and video, then you are opening the program, you are opening new projects or going to old and doing certain functions within. Each time that occurs, it is showing within the pathway that I am opening this and going to this to open this. And, of course, point A to B, B to C, C to D, and D to E and of course, that becomes noticed as a pattern in the computer. And once that is all that's done, then a superhighway is built from the point A through the point E.

Your mind does the same in associated thought. I am a useless person. One pathway is built. I am a useless person. Two pathways are built next to one another. By the 1000th I am a worthless person. You have built 100 highways next to one another that are so close it is turned into one large wide highway.

This gives your thought the mental ability to fly through the highway. There's no stopping to ask for directions. There is no should I turn left here or right here. It is simply point A to B, then B to C, and C to D, and D to E, and now it is finished. Your thoughts have greater ease revisiting those things that you already understand and will do so mechanically through your body if you allow that energy to occur.

If you set your consciousness more so to the autopilot by being disengaged with your experience in that now moment you are setting the autopilot.

If you set your consciousness more so to the autopilot by being disengaged with your experience in that now moment you are setting the autopilot. You are allowing the superhighway to take those previous repetitive thoughts and now it is burnt into your psychology permanently.

Now you are in fact worthless. Not because you are actually worthless, but because your belief is ingrained inside of your consciousness so deeply it's a burn. There is extreme processes that occur to break apart that highway or to build new ones that are better for you to go through or more convenient to go through.

This is why it is important through the traumas of sexuality to understand the nature of the truth behind the Soul essence, not the story that is told to yourself repetitively that created the way that you feel about that experience. The way that you open your experience to start with and the way the pain carries automatically, because you have built a thought highway, which builds an emotional highway, which builds a consciousness highway, which diverts when upon autopilot and registers only what you thought, felt and see about that experience before.

This construct alone is where the trauma becomes a natural portion of your own consciousness and does so because you repetitively allow that energy to go.

This in and of itself is what is known as self-perpetuating trauma. This construct alone is where the trauma becomes a natural portion of your own consciousness and does so because you repetitively allow that energy to go. So, of course, the easiest thought in your next moment is to perpetuate the same form of repetitive energies that you have incurred throughout your time.

Now we understand as your human experience goes through trauma there will always be forms of confusion. There will always be a way to work from the level of where you understand in this moment to where you can start unlocking and reversing these traumas. And although we will share many great things in our next interaction with all of you, we will share this in this moment.

There is a way to reroute your natural highways of thought and emotions in the consciousness that is within the energy of your traumas.

There is a way to help reroute psychology. There is a way to reroute emotional responses. There is a way to reroute your natural highways of thought and emotions in the consciousness that is within the energy of your traumas.

These are the things we will share the next time. We will express to you how best that it is to work with hidden traumas, how best it is to work with mental and emotional traumas, how best to work with clearing the forms of resistance and traumas that have occurred through the auspice of energy and through repetition in experiencing itself. And, of course, we will share techniques to do this as well.

We wish to bid all of you adieu. But before we disconnect, we will share this. Through the experience of traumas that have been instilled upon you, that have been a part of your own experience as a Soul, the amount of power that is given to those resistances can of course be worked with deeply and internally.

As all of our consciousness works as a greater form of oneness in our collective energy, we can understand the mapping of these consciousnesses as we meet every human that we have co-created with not only in this time that is your now movement, but also 17,000 B.C. when working with the Egyptian Consciousness. Also in 4000 B.C. as we worked in South American Consciousness. Also in India at 28,000 B.C. and in all regions of the world in which we have co-created with humans.

The one thing that we do understand is the nature of how resistance can be experienced by the vast majority of all humans upon Earth. Reminding yourself that because all of us are one, that if you feel trauma that feels very specific to your experience, all entities in the universe hold a piece of that trauma as well. Clearing their trauma helps you clear yours and you clearing yours helps others clear theirs as well.

When a collective of our own energy works with you to clear the traumas that are within us all then, of course, we are giving that same gift to the universe.

We congratulate all of you for your growth, and we thank you for ours. We will bid you adieu for this day. And, of course, you are loved.

Greetings to all this is Aridif. That is A R I D I F. And this is it spelled. We understand that all of you are here to connect with the constructs, which we have shared previously to this day, but before diving into those queries, there are, of course, two things that we wish to express. The first thing above and beyond all things that are expressed in this day to know, perceive and to experience and feel that you are loved in our perspective is of the utmost importance. And secondly, it is truly our greatest excitement to co-create with all of you in this moment.

The singular, independent, co-creative, collective consciousness and of the co-created, co-creation of the collective form of our intermediate consciousness of co-creation and intermediate vicinity of co-creator collective consciousness and not bound by that linear time perspective as well. So, of course, we will take your queries at your leisure.

Thank you very much, Aridif.

Yes, of course.

You discussed the slow poison of societal messaging in your third transmission. You also mentioned that those messages are deceitful. Can you speak to the level of consciousness behind those deceitful messages and the underlying motivation that propagates them?

Yes, of course. First of all, there are multitudes of levels in which these messages occur. The first portion and that which is the most and least form of harmfulness in one co-creation is that of the understanding of the human collective at the moment of co-creating with another. Of course, the larger programming for the human collective has already taken its effect. So of course, those who have been integrated and inundated with all of this energy from the time they've been birthed until they are going through transition of understanding that what they are experiencing around them is not a co-creation of their own desire.

That is the energy in which one person will shame another within their own social circle, friendship, family, etc. and these can be the most personally harmful for the human who is experiencing the shame, the human who is experiencing the judgment. But is the least harmful in the intention behind that construct.

The intention alone for most entities is simply to make sure that you are aware of what others would think, how others would perceive, or a simple judgment coming from the internal portion of that person due to their own resistances and own traumas that were experienced. In this way, the intention is not to destroy the mindset, the emotional complexity, or the co-creational form of energy between one person and their dear friend, relative, family, etc. But only as a part of that last layer do most of the co-creations happen.

Go to the opposite end of the spectrum and one that is in the worst aspect of malevolence and one that is co-created from a place and a desire to perceive separation in that same collective form. Now this occurs also on multiple levels. This occurs with the corporations who understand that if you feel negative about yourself, then you buy a product in order to feel better about yourself, to perceive the social animal that you are, and receiving that acceptance from all entities within your circle, of course, you must buy the product at hand.

But higher forms of malevolence still exist in those same forms of corporations and those that own. What most humans would call entities that are perceived as elite. There are some of these humans who perceive that they understand the nature of human experience better than the simple and dumb humans at the bottom. And, of course, with that form of hubris will try to twist the world to their own design.

What their own mind believes that the world should be, will be their co-creational form. And, of course, further still with the forms of malevolence entities that are of negative consequence from the human perspective, those that are type two and highly malevolent have worked with other beings that work in co-creation of human form and teach the tools of manipulation to these entities and also teach them to other humans that are within that elite era and have psychic or physical contact with them.

But more than this, the nature of this co-creation from the very birthing place is the co-creative collective human consciousness and the Earth Collective itself that desired to have an experience that was an experience of adversity, experience of a great deal of suppression and a great deal of oppression in order to experience finding your way out of this.

It is just as all of you who go to your haunted houses in Halloween season. You enter knowing that it will be a very large fright to you. You understand there will be discomfort, fear, adrenaline, and all of the consequences of being scared from your wits. But yet you engage and buy that ticket. You see the Scary Movie. You watch the play in which the murderer roams loose because that part of the experience tells you something about yourself.

And the Earth Collective Consciousness from the core depth of that energy of course, is an experience that all entities upon the Earth Collective from the very beginning of your Earth Incarnation Cycle, of the first-density energy and your second-density bacterial constructs until the KunKae were the first third density race. And to the furthest reach of future humans and whatever race may appear after from your linear time perspective. All of you have desired to feel this experience.

And of course, with that experience brought the opportunity for creation at hand in such a way. And although it is the most difficult prospect of being the human incarnation to overcome sexual adversity, mental adversity, emotional adversity, and all things intertwined, it is one that teaches your Soul at the greatest level of course.

Thank you, Aridif.

Yes, of course.

You discuss the connection between thought, beliefs, and emotions. You also discussed what you described as superhighways of patterning that can be created in the human mind and nervous system. And finally, you share that sexual trauma exists in the very template of the human collective consciousness. That all incarnating humans come in with some form of sexual trauma on account of this. The question is, does the human collective consciousness have something akin to a neural network like the human brain does? And can certain beliefs create similar superhighways at the collective level?

Yes, of course. Now, if you are looking at this energy as a pure collective consciousness. Yes, of course. All beliefs that are en masse beliefs in the Earth Collective Consciousness and that are the greater form of co-created beliefs. Then of course this can create a form of the neural transmission or the superhighway of consciousness, the reiteration of the continuous, consecutive, highly sought, highly thought, and highly expressed thoughts and beliefs. Of course, that energy then creates an opportunity for all entities who wish to be a part of that collective, who hold the mindset, emotional set, and energetic setting to be within that co-creative field and attach to that energy purely.

Now, if you are looking at the level of the personal form of the human collective, this is done more so through the forms of epigenetics and through the forms of simple vibrational learning. As we've expressed previously as a human is born into the world, the first emotions that are laid into their chakra system are the mother's pushing through that canal and in most, as humans perceive, Western forms of society this birth comes with great pain.

This birth comes with the great trauma and emotional feeling of imbalance of fear for the child's safety, for fear for their own safety. The father, mother, or other parent that is there also fearing, the doctor concerned, but unempathetic nurses trying to create experience of rushing you through that door in order to get to the next patient who comes, and the entire hospital, sitting as an overlay of energy.

Where, just upstairs, someone was burned near death and knows they will never walk again. Never speak again. Never close their eyelids again as they are horrifically and horribly mutated within their own physical construct. The child that has died downstairs in the Children's Cancer Ward. And all that energy is bombarding this new consciousness and Soul. So, of course, it is not hard to perceive in that way. That once the human enters the Earth Collective Consciousness and the energetic properties of others are its first teachers. Then what energy is being taught to that human first?

The times in which we have perceived the least form of sexual resistance in the majority of humans are in countries and areas that either operate near indigenous forms of levels where birth is natural. And done so around those that are loved. Fairly to no pain that accompanies. As well as a great support system of those that are excited, happy, joyous of that moment. But of course, continues as that child grows.

So these forms of indigenous entities would not be in a place where starvation occurs. These entities that hold smaller amounts of sexual trauma would not be in environments where animals could easily eat or attack them. These entities would be in extremely safe areas because the vibrational learning that occurs for the first three to five years would be that of the most resistant free environment for the human possible.

But even then as the human grows, as more entities leave that village and meet new humans and bring back new humans into their village of course that energy is repetitive. But even these entities through generations have had their village attacked by others, the feminine entities raped, the masculine entities killed, and this energy embeds in the epigenetics as well.

So, no human is immune from that form of resistance. But there are greater and lesser forms pending upon that person, pending upon their vibrational learning state and, of course, pending upon their own personal interactivity with the world. How they perceive, receive, and how they share their own consciousness with others. All of these things play an extremely different role, and yet all are vitally important for the formula that equates to how well one works in the world and how little or much resistance in their sexuality and in all of their fields that occurs as well.

Thank you very much, Aridif.

Yes, of course.

The next question is from an individual who took your advice from the last question and answer session specifically about disconnecting and getting some distance from the hybridization process and also using the technique that you suggested for protection and non-interference.

She explains that she expressed her intention to disconnect her lower fractal from the hybridization process and to use the technique for protection and non-interference that you suggested with the intention that she would not give any entity her fear. Later that evening she had a sensation of extreme pressure throughout her pelvis, like someone was sitting on her. But it felt intensely magnetic, like trying to keep two magnets apart. She also shares that she had an experience of a male entity trying to be sexual with her, but who was unable to do so. Can you speak to this experience and was this experience connected to your transmissions and the work through this course?

Yes, of course. First of all, as you are perceiving the co-creation at hand, as you are feeling these energies as they work with your body through both physical and energetic levels, yes of course. Your intention, your direct work, the co-creation with your Higher Fractal Consciousness, and your desire to protect yourself in working with that form of disconnection from all experiences in that energy of the hybridization program and sexual relations that are not authorized by your own consciousness, that are not desired, or simply the utilization of your DNA in nonsexual things. All of this is taken greatly into account by the Higher Fractal Consciousness.

As it is, there's a part of your co-creative sphere, as a larger part of your own self, as a support system for yourself. So of course, they worked with your consciousness to divert the experience of that which exists in your astral projected state and removed all attachment of that focus of consciousness into that co-creation.

The experience that you are feeling in the pelvis region was a diversion from your physical layer working with that energy that is directly related to your sexual reproductive organs and done so through all layers. Now mind you in this energy the format of what we've expressed, of course, that DNA which is taken, is often taken from the higher dimensional form and rarely occurs in your physical state.

Yet when consciousness connects your own energy throughout all dimensions your physical attributes are connected. The hand that exists on the end of your wrist is still the hand that exists in the higher dimension. Simply a higher dimensional form. The fingers that exist in your higher dimensional form still exist in the next level of higher dimension and so on, etc. Your reproductive organs are the same.

So as they are disconnecting quite literally, that physical attribute in your dimensional state to not allow the co-creational field experience of reproducing in the lowest of dimensional form. That is the magnetism that you are feeling, the chakra directly disconnecting from sexual co-creation in another state.

This why the entity that approaches you in desire of sexual congress is not allowed to co-create because your lower astral body, your physical fourth-density and third-density body refuses that co-creational experience. So it is not allowed to co-create with you in that way. It is not allowed to bring forward its own sexuality with yours and that part of your experience no longer exists.

Now, of course, if there are ever terms in the future in which you desire to co-create with specific entities in that way, to express love through the sexual attributes of your own consciousness, of course, this is your case-by-case basis, and will still work with any entity that you desire co-creation from.

But you should not experience that energy being projected upon you. You should not experience that energy in a co-creative manner that feels your free will left out of that decision. And if that energy ever were to occur simply repeat that process.

Now, of course, we have had entities that we worked with in the time of your ancient Egyptian consciousness and humans that we worked with in sleep states in that same area and time region. These entities would experience the construct of similar energies although not through hybridization directly. Simply astral states entities that are reptilian in nature and earthbound in nature. And their co-creation came from a level of their own spirituality. A celebration of the reptilian form of energy, but a disconnect from the intensive form of violent sexuality that occurs with some forms of reptilian consciousness.

So, of course, there was the pull back and forth of desire to be more divine, a desire to feel divinity through sexuality, but a lack of desire to work with that construct. So what would occur? They would create separation through their Higher Fractal Consciousness, through terms of their own understanding and sever that tie.

But the excitement to feel divinity and excitement to feel reptilian sexual co-creation brought back that energy. It was indecisive in that way. And indecisiveness within the co-creation of that energy will bring about the back and forth. Make sure this is what you desire to separate. And if you desire to change your mind you are not limited to that concept, either.

Thank you so much, Aridif.

Yes, of course.

And what a beautiful example of the Higher Fractal Consciousness, as you suggested, I guess for lack of better terms, respecting the wishes and the free will of the lower fractal.

Yes, of course. That energy is a vitally important part of the human collective working with the Higher Fractal Consciousness as it is a component of your own consciousness, but one that has independent co-creative desires as well.

Thank you. The next question is how would you suggest that men and women best work with the rise of the divine feminine energies on the planet.

Yes, of course, now we understand that there's a different intention from one human to the next in why they would perceive. This should be a construct of their own. One that simply feels that the feminine energy is quite foreign to them and wonders the best way to work for that energy. And yet another that holds a masculine body and does not feel the feminine energy inside of themselves. Around themselves.

And yet there are others who hold masculine energy and feel persecuted for that energy as well. All three of these have quite different answers, of course. Those who do not understand feminine energy simply look inside of yourself for that which is feminine. This is where most humans hold a great deal of confusion for the construct of energy that is received from yourself, from your Higher Fractal Consciousness, and from various other layers of the internal consciousness.

What exists inside of yourself that receive all forms of energy is that of the feminine. Or which feels the desire to co-create nurturing and love from a greatly emotional heart-centric nature is that of your feminine energy. In either of those humans who feel they do not understand, they simply must understand this portion of their own consciousness. All of you have this within you. All of you feel that energy.

Secondly, those who wish to understand the nature of integration that in the feminine form of energy and do not feel connected to that form of energy. It is a simple, energetic exercise to simply feel the feminine energy from those that you love the most.

Some of you hold no relationships with feminine entities and are in masculine bodies. Some of the reasons why this occurs is that there is a feeling inside of you of a disliking or hatred for the feminine energy. This has to do with wounds that exist within your co-creative sphere. Traumas that existed within those wounds from your co-creative sphere. Or simply not co-creating with the form of feminine energy that resonated with you enough to feel that bond. Even still, we would dare to say that nearly all humans that exist hold love for an entity that exists within feminine consciousness.

Some of you hold a masculine form of energy and do not co-create with feminine entities upon the co-creation of the Earth Collective Consciousness, yet you will listen to those who are feminine Pleiadian beings speak nearly every moment. And each moment you hear the sharing from those entities your heart opens. Connect with that form of feminine energy.

When you are connecting with your pets, one entity that is specifically able to receive and nurture, even those that are feminine bodies open your heart to that. You must start somewhere with that experience. You must be open to understanding the nature of the resistance and the trauma in yourself that co-creates feelings of misgiving.

Now, of course, those of you in the last category simply feel as if you are persecuted for holding masculine energy. Now, of course, we understand the nature of that expression from your human perspective as well as we perceive the collective consciousness. And what you are being exposed to that makes you feel as if this is co-creation that is highly important, is a very small minority of humans who simply do not like entities that are in masculine bodies.

And, of course, the same that is expressed with those who hold no affection, love, or care for those who are in feminine bodies. So this form is a great sense of discrimination that is sexist and nearly to the point of racism in the construct that is the race of that which is feminine, the race of that which is masculine. Now we understand that you do not divide by race within this planet. But the construct holds concretely between the co-creants between that energy and your experience elsewhere.

So, of course, the energy is a small minority of entities. And you have chosen to listen to those entities as a representative of your Earth Collective about how entities feel about your masculine energy. There's a reason that you do this as well. There is a part of your own consciousness, a part of your subconscious, a part of your traumatized human version that perceives a judgment toward your own masculine energy.

That is what angers you so greatly. There's a part of you that fears if they are correct, that if masculine beings are not acceptable, that if masculine things that are done through the name of masculinity are toxic itself. Now when you are perceiving that consciousness, what you are perceiving is a part of the collective that has divided greatly these terms. Just as you have felt internally dividing your own consciousness.

Even though you hold a form of masculine energy that is higher on average than the majority of humans. This does not make you negative, or bad, or disconnected from the human collective in any form. What this does is hold an energy inside of you that allows you to experience that energy more drastically and more fiercely than others.

But when you are working with that energy, understanding what a divine masculinity is versus simple human understanding of what masculinity is are two different constructs altogether. In order to not hold resistance against your sexuality, the simple masculine form of energy energetically in your second chakra and with a part of your own energy that burns with desire and burns to create and to give others from your internal self, this is the portion of masculinity that needs to be perceived.

And if this holds imbalance, then of course the form of human collective will perceive it in much greater light. And perceive it as that toxic forms of masculinity. As long as you are truly honoring yourself, truly honoring the masculine and feminine energy within you, then all humans that are together and apart will not affect you unless you allow that feeling.

Thank you very much, Aridif. That makes a lot of sense.

Yes, of course.

Another question is, are sexual desires such as kinks or fetishes developed due to an internal imbalance, or does your Soul personality play a part in it? And would it be possible to change it just like you change any other belief system, or is it healthier to accept it?

Yes. Now, of course, we have shared this construct previously to some degree that within what humans call kinks and what they perceive holds a great deal of many layers of energy. Some of these that are developed through traumas. Some that are developed through the natural construct of sexuality and growth in the human form. But many times it is where the wires are crossed.

Now, in that way, humans who hold feelings of positive, responsive, sexual energy but are told through that co-created collective format that the feelings of sexuality, that who felt were inappropriate. Then, of course, this creates that form of taboo inside of you. And that form of taboo felt good to you. But now you must hide it away from others.

Of course, when you are feeling sexual co-creation with another while you are sleeping and they did not receive permission from you, if you felt that stimulating and it excites you and holds that level of what kink is to yourself, then of course you feel guilty about that energy. Yet in co-creation of energy that you are experiencing the only way that you are able to experience that in co-creational form is to work through that in a healthy co-creation. That a kink is not one that is negative. That kink does hold components that which is against your free will.

But if you're desiring a co-creation of that form, and consent is the cornerstone of free will, then, of course, many things can be done. Expressing to your sexual partner that you wish for them to surprise you with sexuality during your sleeping state.

Now, of course, this is seen as uncommon and disturbing by many. Yet, if your partner desires to co-create that sensation with yourself and you yourself desire that co-creation and no free will is taken then of course that energy is important and should be acted upon with your desire and acceptance of that energy.

Now, of course, energies that are within kinks that become harmful. This is another portion of energy that we have shared previously as well. Diverting that construct. Taking others' free will of utilizing your form of free will must be accepted. This energy is important for you to change and burdensome, yes. Kinks that are healthy and kinks that are unhealthy both can be shifted and shifted quite easily.

The experience of sexuality comes through the arousal of one's energetic properties. Second chakra. Physical body. Genitals. Etc. During an act of co-creation or self-touching in that way. And both can be experienced not only when you are willing to work with new concepts of your own sexuality, new co-creation with others of your sexuality, and working through finding that new form of excitement that brings you the same level of thrill of that of the previous energy.

Now, of course, we will share a very simple and very innocent example of this. If your own energy desires a certain body part to rub against your genitals, as it were, and that energy excites you the most, then of course, that energy can be fulfilled quite easily. But if your desire is to do so when someone is not under the awareness of that energy by simply bumping into them, then of course you have taken that entity's free will away.

The energy of your own consciousness is to shift that out of the energy. Understanding that when you are working against another's free will of course you are simply taking more resistance from your collective, from yourself, from the area of your sexuality, the second chakra, heart chakra, etc. and adding resistances to that energy. So shifting over the removal of another's free will, and shifting it over simply to the co-creation with those that are willing co-creants and those that are willing consentful co-creation partners in that way.

Moving through another form of finding a new kink. Finding new energy that is potent through arousal is a very important process. For example, if your sexual preference is that either you or your partner are on top and the other is upon the bottom, and that is the only way you have operated, and each time that you have stepped away from the model that you are using, it was not a comfortable co-creation.

So, what would change in your experience? Of course, creating a feeling. A desire to shift that energy. Allowing your body to relax in the co-creation. Allowing your mind not to focus on the reasons why you have deemed the regulation that you must be either upon the top or bottom. And allow the partner to co-create with you in a way that is opposite.

And if that becomes so uncomfortable that you cannot work through it, then of course step away from that energy as it will not help you co-create a new form. Then change into something that is different. Something that you have not done. That your partner and yourself or simply yourself are willing to try. And go through a great deal of the mental checklists until you are able to find that one thing that brings a level of arousal.

That is so much further higher from the others that it becomes your new going to preference for sexuality. Now, of course, these are not the only ways to work through, but these are the most third-dimensional ways to work through that energy.

If there's a kink that you find harmful to yourself or to the free will of others, simply meditate. And in your co-creation of your second chakra clear resistance by visualizing yourself pushing the energy out of your second chakra and into the earth. Then visualize yourself breathing in the Earth energy into your second chakra. And then breathe your heart chakra into your second chakra as well.

Sit there for multiple moments feeling the turning and churning of your second chakra's energy. Feels as it starts stimulating outward and start feeling the energy of that old kink leave as the energy resistance that created the area for the first place or that traumatic form of experience that created that in the first place.

Use your mind as well. Visualize the thought form itself leaving your mind, leaving your heart, leaving the sacral chakra and leaving your experience altogether.

Thank you very much, Aridif.

Yes, of course.

You spoke in the latest transmission about some of the causes of sexual trauma and some of the forms of abuse that can lead to it. And could you speak to the entities who are the perpetrators in that? Do they continue predatory behavior in being an abuser after they have completed their current lifetime? And if so, how does that energy persist after an entity is passed?

Yes, of course. Now, first of all, this can occur, yes. But rarely occurs in that way that humans perceive. Most humans who leave the incarnation cycle and go into the afterlife cycle only carry forms of resistance in a long-term sense that are highly resistant in their experience and in their life theme.

For example, those humans who have been sexually hurt and sexually traumatized, those that were raped, and those that are experiencing human forms of trafficking, these entities will hold sexual trauma. And it will exist even after the experience of leaving the human body until they have allowed their consciousness to focus on the releasing of that energy.

Most humans perceive that after their physical death experience that all things that were resistant to them will dissipate and disappear. And it can work in that way, but seldomly does for the human energy. It is a process. And linear time does not exist nearly in the rapidity or frequency that it will in the fifth and sixth density. But exists nothing as it does in human terms as well.

Many humans may go through the experience of experiencing one hundred years of time experience. But do so in one day. Other humans, who have left the physical plain long enough, are able to feel an experience of ten minutes that linearly upon the Earth's time passage would be ten years. So of course, all of these energies are important to perceive of the level of that energy.

Now, those who are an aggressor, those who are an abuser, these entities hold naturally much higher levels of resistance. Most entities who were victimized and traumatized but never utilized that pain and suffering to turn on others are already equipped with that energy inside of themselves to start working upon that healing much more quickly.

But to those who decided to take the pain that was given to them and utilize that as a tool to hurt others that they felt in more control or felt more dominant over the world or whatever terms their co-creational field, mentality, psychology, and mind took them. Then, of course, the energy becomes much more resistant and much more dangerous within the co-creation of other entities upon that afterlife experience.

Just as humans you would not wish to have a rapist within your home, so too in the afterlife do not wish to have a Soul that is an offender in that way being within your proximity or energy. And within the level of those entities that are human extremely rare cases of that exist for multiple years.

Most of the time that experience that feels as if it were decades, hundreds, or, in extremely rare cases, thousands of years which go by in a short time in human terms so as not to involve the humans that exist in that realm. As freshly after going into that realm of consciousness, you are still extremely close to the human collective form and then able to work with humans on a more physical level.

You see this many times in your collective with those that are shadow people. You see this with the cold feeling entities of co-creation. Yet most entities who wish to sexually form traumatization upon humans in that term are from a lower fourth density, astral projected state. And now humans are perceiving these consciousnesses less because you yourself are entering fourth density.

So, as they are consciousnesses much lower than that of the average fourth-density entity you would have been able to experience that more so in your co-creational field of your dreamstates of third density ten years previous than you would in this time in your timeline lineage.

Now, of course, we have shared with all of you what it is to co-create protection for yourself, what it is to not hold traumas and co-create with those that hold similar or much worse traumas.

And we have also shared the protectionary construct in which holds frequency of protecting that aspect of yourself.

But it is important for those who've felt the experience of consciousnesses and Souls that would physically try to harm them in astral projected dream states or that would co-create forms of rape within the sleep state then of course separating your consciousness from that layer of the dream state and from the energy by protecting it can be of great use to you.

But also, as you are transitioning from your own energies and your own resistances, your own traumas, your own internal co-creational constructs. This places you outside of that co-creational field at much higher percentage layers. But working with that protectionary layer, of course, is one of the greater terms to success for a deviation of all acts of experience for that.

Thank you very much, Aridif.

Yes, of course.

Looking at the full spectrum of this and speaking of folks who have experienced sexual abuse and for whom sexuality has not really been connected to love, can you speak some more to the relationship between love, pleasure, and sex? And could you share the best way to move into a frequency of love if that is not been the basis and expression of your sexuality previously?

Yes, of course. Now as we have shared that near our introduction of sexuality with a human collective at this time. Through Rob's own energy and sharing in the way that we are in this moment. We have first shared about sexuality that you do not have to love the person in a way of marriage, you do not have to love the person as if you desire for them to be the partner for eternity as this is a construct that is very conditional to the way that you perceive or believe that relationships should or should not be.

Those that are monogamous benefit from that feeling. Those that are polyamorous may not, but the appreciate form of co-creation with another and simple appreciation of their own consciousness is enough to work with moving towards love energy.

And what we mean if you are having sexual engagement with multiple partners. And you seem to not notice who or what they are. You are highly disconnecting your heart from that area. And of course, this is not of a negative consequence specifically for the desired outcome of your experience, but you can only greatly benefit from the experience of moving more of that heart energy into your sexuality and fulfill more of your experience as a human.

So, of course, what is the first level of love? I appreciate you as a human being. What is the next step? I like you as a human being. And what is the next level? I care for you as a human being. You are an acquaintance. And what is the next level? You are a friend. What is the next? You are a dear friend. What is next? You are beloved to me.

Each progression towards that energy does not experience a requirement for you to have sexuality and to not gain levels of resistance in higher and perpetuating amounts. But the more energy that you bring from the heart, the lesser forms of disconnection that you will have if you are not engaging, at minimal, that I care for you as you as a human being. Then you will bring forms of that energy in resistance towards the co-creation of yourself.

Now, of course, those who have held forms of trauma that were done to you, of course. This becomes a safety component of your physical body safety just as much as your emotional protection for not desiring to get too close to other humans. So, it would be important to start trying to develop friendships without sexuality. To start developing personal or intimate conversations with those friends after they gained your trust after you have built a co-creation with them in that fashion.

But it is also important after that time has gone, even if it is highly uncomfortable for you at the beginning, to start allowing others to be intimate with yourself. That is the barrier that most humans who hold either experiences of sexual trauma or high levels of resistance inside of their experience from experiences of sexual trauma cannot overcome. That is a threshold they cannot pass. That is an energy they will not acquaint themselves with. Allowing others to be intimate with them.

We do not mean sexual intimacy as we have expressed previously, although it can form in that way. What we are sharing is the intimacy of truly knowing another. Now we understand to know another human being you need to understand the consciousness that is behind the flesh of the being. That can be done at a lower appreciative level and a very high level of love, endearment, and true connection of heart to heart.

But, the level in which you are able to start must be the level of appreciation from yourself to theirs. If you dare try to simultaneously run your feelings for another and theirs to yours, there will be a requirement, of course, that energy is to be vulnerable with another human being.

This is the part that is the most scary, this is the part that is worst for those that have been victimized because most of you who were victimized by an entity were ones that you trusted. Ones that who dared love, ones that you opened yourself from friendship to great love upon.

Now, of course, we know this is not all humans. That there are versions of that energy that were from humans you did not know or were not aware of or simply had just met in that time. Many of you who hold deeper levels of trauma from greater forms of tragedies were harmed by those who should not have been in a position to instill that harm upon you. Such as those that are family members, such as those that are parents, such as those that are beloved uncles, aunts, and cousins to you. Brothers and sisters. But the energy of intimacy is highly important and it is highly important form to go both ways as well.

Thank you so much, Aridif. And thank you for taking so much time with us. I'm wondering if there is time for one final question for this session?

Yes, of course, we will take your final query. Yes.

Thank you, Aridif. This individual says that phallus praying goes back to the times of the god Shiva and the yoni temple derives from his wife Parvati. And is asking who are the gods Shiva and Parvati and why are they depicted as having blue skin. And if this is accurate, what is the connection between the phallus and the yoni and these beings?

Yes, of course. Now, in the co-creation of these entities there are many depictions of entities that were and had blue skin. And, of course, some of those that you have seen in cave drawings, some of those that you have perceived in your world affairs were from our own race as fifth-density entities as we created avatars physically to co-create with humans upon the level when humans allowed other races to come. And from their perspective, the gods to co-create in that way. And when we were invited to the Earth Collective, we would take form and co-create in that way.

The entities that were, for the most part, Hindu gods were multitudes of races. The specific entities and deities that you are speaking of were a collective consciousness of Arcturian and humanoid co-created hybrids for lack of better terms. That which is deemed Krishna was an appropriate form of Pleiadian and Arcturian hybrid in that way, with the human forms of DNA that was creating with the Earth Collective Consciousness for teaching and for the Christic consciousness collective co-creant. So there are multitudes of energies that deal with these consciousnesses.

Most entities who perceived Shiva, perceived Shiva through multitudes of generations and did so because they were multiple different entities from multiple different races. The shiva lingam and the co-creant counterpart of this energy were, of course, the co-creation of the sexuality within these entities as it was not uncommon for those that were of Type Two nature to work in sexuality with humans, either in a direct physical form or by showing them with their actual body parts. As there was no shame for nudity in the time, place, and region, and there were no concerns of what a nude body appeared.

So, these entities would either sexually co-create with humans in that way or to show them through their own sexuality different forms of techniques that could allow a co-creation for humans to start letting go of their own resistances as in those time periods were post Annunaki co-creations. Were understood and known that humans held sexual trauma. And when co-creating with other consciousnesses, it was highly important for them to teach you how to release that sexual resistance and trauma as well. How beautiful.

Thank you so much.

Yes, of course.

And thank you as always, for your love and support and energy for answering these queries for the folks who are taking the course now and who will be hearing these materials and going through this journey in the future.

Yes, of course. We wish to express to all of you and as you are going through the experience of finding the resistances that exist inside of you, when you go through the experience of knowing traumas that were in your past and finding new ways to work with that energy, when most of you are going through some form of shift in your internal energy.

Remember, that as we have expressed, working with your heart, connecting the second chakra to the heart chakra is very important working with the energetic portions of your consciousness with the forms of tools and visualizations are also very important additions to the co-creational field of energy between. And knowing that your own form of co-creation with sexuality either internally to yourself or with a partner must be expressed in the least resistant fashion that is possible. All of you are working towards a co-creation of that energy.

Many of you have shifted great deals of internal energies surrounding one event in your experience or one part of your consciousness that was more resistant than others. We wish to congratulate all of you for that growth. We wish to thank all of you for the growth you are giving us in the co-creation of energetic comprisal of this entire collective energy. As you are aware when one grows, all grow. And we thank you for this. Adieu.

G reetings to all this is Aridif. That is A R I D I F and this is it spelled. We understand that you desire to finalize the construct in which we have been sharing. The construct that surrounds the human consciousness around the idea of sexuality, trauma that is invested from sexuality, trauma that is repercussion of sexuality, and trauma that is very deeply interwoven with human sexuality. You wish to understand why it occurs, how it occurs, where it occurs, in what levels of consciousness outside of Earth does it occur. And we feel we have shared the basic construct with all of you on these topics.

But the one thing that we have not fully shared how to work with the energy in which you have from the place of resistances and, of course, the place of traumas in which all of you experience sexuality for the most part. Now, of course, we will share a great deal of things that are important to do with sexuality around the entirety of the subject, both in trauma removal and self-observation.

But before diving into this construct, we will express the two things that we feel are most important out of all things that we have shared within the entire topic that we share. The most important thing from our own perspective is that you know, feel, and perceive that you are loved. And when you love another entity, of course, this is one consciousness. One consciousness that is divided, that is a separate segregated entity that shares an emotion with yet another separate and segregated entity.

But when you are loved all entities that are within the universal construct that are created from the essence of love itself hold a connection of oneness with you. Entities that are in your guidance centers love you. Entities that are part of your Oversoul. Entities and beings that you have never co-created with, met, nor will in this entire experience and lifetime love you. And because all of these entities and the universe itself and the core essence of your own consciousness truly and unconditionally love you. Then, of course, instead of us loving you, you are loved.

And the second that is important in this co-creation is that this is truly our greatest excitement, not only in this moment, but through all moments of your linear time perspective.

First of all, how do you know where your trauma is? How do you understand the nature of your trauma? How do you know if it is hidden in subconscious and unconscious layers that are beneath your awareness?

First of all, there must be an idea, energy in where your trauma comes from to understand if it is hidden or if it is not.

First of all, there must be an idea, energy in where your trauma comes from to understand if it is hidden or if it is not.

Many of you remember an act at hand, an experience at hand, a co-creation at hand, but do not recall or feel or are co-created with an energetic or overwhelming feeling of trauma. Yet it exists within you nonetheless.

Many of you understand and know the nature of an experience that felt bad out of the moment but pass it off as if it were just part of life and that experience. Not knowing if the traumas held to your consciousness at some level. And, of course, we will share with the majority of you, of course, that trauma still remains. And it remains within a multitude of systems that are within yourself. The mental body, emotional body, your subconscious, unconscious, your physical body, your chakra system, your etheric body, auric field.

All of these hold trauma that are dealing with sexual co-creation and sexual relations with a majority of human beings and the majority of sexual experiences.

All of these hold trauma that are dealing with sexual co-creation and sexual relations with a majority of human beings and the majority of sexual experiences. Remaining in those very few that tend to feel healing at the moment are held with trauma within the human consciousness.

Now, when we express those sexual experiences that create healing, what we do not mean is your sexual frustration led you to random co-creation with a person. And after the release of your sexual pent energy exploding through your second chakra, either the masculine form release from the penis directly outward or from the feminine form reverberated outward into the auric field and beyond. What we mean is a true form of sexual creation or co-creation that truly allows your Soul to feel letting go of resistance. That chips away at that part of resistance and, of course, the trauma that is held within.

Humans hold trauma very deeply, as if you are a river flowing, something is starting to clog that river. And we understand we have used this analogy previously, but if you do not clear this pathway, the energy of the consciousness cannot flow. This is why a majority of humans work with severe problematic forms of first chakra resistance and energy. And that is due to the nature of your second chakra holding the energy from going into that first chakra in full flow. And, of course, the energy that is within the third chakra mostly holds resistance for the majority of humans. And, of course, the heart chakra.

This is not abnormal for third-density entities, but it is abnormal from those who are going from third to fourth as humans are in this third-to-fourth density exchange.

This is not abnormal for third-density entities, but it is abnormal from those who are going from third-to-fourth as humans are in this third to fourth density exchange. Now, in that way, some of these beliefs that you hold create a feeling for you that expresses that through all sexual experience, who did not in fact hold, receive, or experience trauma. Yet the trauma remains within you.

Some of you hold belief systems that say that sexual trauma is an ordinary part of the human consciousness, and although this is correct within our observation it does not have to be correct for the Creator at hand. It can be an experience that allows releasing of that experience from trauma within your physical body structure and your energetic fields and properties respectively.

The energy of your body can release this construct with those positive sexual experiences.

The energy of your body can release this construct with those positive sexual experiences. And when we express those that are positive and healing, what we mean and give in great example is that entity that you love dearly, that you co-create with frequently. Friend, lover, partner, husband or wife, this entity and you have gone through a great deal of sexual trauma as in nearly all relationships in the human realm.

But in one day of release all of your inhibitions, all of your fear, all of your resistance to the ties of emotions and problems that may have occurred within your linear relationship and truly allowed your heart consciousnesses to mix with one another and your bodies to fulfill the urges physically that they desire. This can be one part of healing.

Now we understand the nature of some of the expressions that we share may feel as if it were taboo in a way, but even that which is a masculine or feminine form who is not engaged sexually but feels extraordinarily sexual and cannot find a mate or partner to co-create this with can find an entity whose job it is to have sex with those who would pay or prostitutes in your terms and have a sexual night with this entity and hold great opening from pain and suffering that did exist previously. But allowed the heart to open to this person as a human being.

Two entities that speak with one another for hours well before getting into the act of sexuality, opening the hearts, the minds, the first, second, and third chakras, and then engaging through sexuality. And if this person who is a prostitute in your terms does not hold a great deal of resistance about their line of work, does not see it as a negative consequence, allows it to be perceived in a way that this person is sharing their own healing with another human. Then both humans can have a healing experience from this experience.

Now, of course, all of the positive sexual interactions are only a portion of how to start working with resistance. But, again, we must find that which is hidden first. Now, going into your hidden constructs and unconscious subconscious layers of energy, it is extremely difficult for the majority of humans to work with that layer as it is unconscious for a reason. As it is subconscious for a reason. These areas do not allow your conscious mind to connect with them. These are the lowest parts of your lower fractal consciousness.

But do not mistake that these parts are the lowest vibrational or the lowest essence of your consciousness. They are simply a divided, compartmentalized mechanism that humans' extreme forms of psychology and extreme forms of difficult and interactive psychology creates in order to have a compartmentalization in an experience that holds spectral vibrations from the most resistance to the least and freest forms of non-resistance.

And with that consciousness going through the worst pain, the greatest joy, within one hour, one day, one year of your experience, there must be a place for this processing to occur that is not within your mental body.

And with that consciousness going through the worst pain, the greatest joy, within one hour, one day, one year of your experience, there must be a place for this processing to occur that is not within your mental body. Humans' mental energy does not allow a depth of co-creation in that way for the majority of these vastly, powerfully energetic experiences. What it does desire is an experience that is focused upon by the entity in that moment.

Being in that very moment that we've shared throughout the time that we have shared with humans, not only in your recent time, but thousands of years and tens of thousands of years previous. As we spoke to human consciousness we shared one of the greater principles of allowing yourself the freedom to manifest and the freedom to not hold resistances and traumas is being in your now moment. So, of course, the subconscious and unconscious are the divided regions of your conscious compartmentalized for the ease and access of living in that Now Moment.

As you experience third density it is frequent experience of your own consciousness shifting backwards and forwards in time, of course, this is extremely normal as it pertains to the human collective energy but all third-density beings throughout the universal consciousness.

And although each galaxy holds a different theme, the third density plays out quite literally in a very similar thread of that experience of exploration of that linear time perspective. Coming from a place of consciousness that only observes the now moment but does not observe history or foresight. Only storing that which did occur in the body as a warning for what comes next.

The second-density consciousness must shift through that time in order to explore fully that realm of consciousness. What can, what could, what will, and want is. And, of course, the third-density consciousness in that exploration also challenges the individual that experiences it to be in that now moment.

So stepping in your now moment is the only way that you are able to deal with the subconscious unconscious layers without additional forms of resistance or inaccessibility.

So stepping in your now moment is the only way that you are able to deal with the subconscious unconscious layers without additional forms of resistance or inaccessibility. Meditation is a focus that we share with all of you that is one of your greater tools to break forward into your consciousness and parts in which you've not yet explored.

Partially, this energy is an allowance of your own consciousness to do what natively it can or should do within your rights of being a sovereign entity and having forms of consciousness expansive from the dimension that you exist through all dimensions of physicality as a multi-dimensional consciousness and holding yourself inside a body. Then, of course, that is your sovereign right as a being to have accessibility of that energy.

But humans do not believe that they can have that consciousness. That they cannot expand into their Higher Fractal Consciousness without some great learnings, some tools of some design. So the meditation is a self-hypnotization that allows you to free yourself from those inhibitions and from the belief systems that hold you as limited consciousness and limited beings.

Meditation is your true allowance to open yourself fully through the freedom and through the auspice of what an unlimited Soul can be experienced as.

Meditation is your true allowance to open yourself fully through the freedom and through the auspice of what an unlimited Soul can be experienced as. So, of course, now you open yourself for the meditation. And what the meditation does, along with the construct of self-hypnotization, it will also allow you to focus upon your Now Moment, to be deeply rooted within yourself, to perceive the layers of consciousness often not perceived because of the resistance to start with.

All of you go into a meditative place and, of course, we highly suggest the grounding technique that Rob has shared with others many times over as a utilization and a preface of all forms of the technique that we share today. If you do not understand or have not been exposed to this technique there's a very simple core that we can share quickly, although the average form of this technique should be utilized within a fifteen minute period.

And that starts with a breathing circuit that creates the inward and outward flow of the breath. And, of course, the breath is the heart chakra expressed into your reality. Both releasing and receiving the heart is your breath. And although the lungs are located around the heart as an organ, the heart chakra experiences that expression deep inside of your chest, radiating from the center area directly right where your heart exists, in the center breastplate of your chest, and radiates out throughout the entirety of the higher body region and the upper quadrants of your body. And as it radiates outward the feeling of that energy is expressed through your breath.

Breathing in allows you to receive love, to receive universal consciousness, to receive the essence of Source itself.

Breathing in allows you to receive love, to receive universal consciousness, to receive the essence of Source itself and that is what we would ask you to visualize in this moment. Is breathing in is receiving Source energy and Source energy manifest for the human understanding better in any way form than utilizing that white light. White light is both a combination of all colors and a rejection of all colors at the same time. The way it is perceived and the way it is reflected are two different consciousnesses.

But the white light is the perfect embodiment of Source energy. And breathe in. As you breathe in through your nose, into your lungs, and stomach, and watch the energy as it goes into your root chakra. And the root chakra is firmly seated at the root of your spinal column. When Rob expresses where this specifically is, he would express that your tailbone near the anus region and, of course, this is accurate and, of course, visualizing the chakra itself is important as well. As you start your breathing circuit.

Preparing yourself for this visualization first. Visualize that root chakra. It is approximately two-thirds of a closed fist in your hand and resides in this region. The color is that of a dark earth red. One that is darker than the forest red that you've perceived. One that is a brown form within the red. One that in its very formation would only invoke the energy of Earth itself to your perspective. That form of red is the one that you perceive and as you're breathing this white light into your nose down to your root chakra, you are transmitting the energy of Source directly into the displacement of the root chakra red energy and allow it to go down into both feet.

And, of course, you will create a pathway for the root chakra to remain in its own sovereignty but still connect to the bottom of your feet and those pathways are known as roots. Roots, or chains, are the perspective that most humans use, utilizing them from your root down both legs simultaneously to the bottom of your feet region. After five to ten breaths, all of the red energy should be transmuted out of your root chakra into the bottom of both feet.

And, of course, at that time we will then displace that red form of energy with more white light coming inward and allowing it to release thirty-three meters deep into your ground. Now, of course, the white light continues to push down that red energy until it finally releases in the Earth.

After that is done, then you bring the golden or green Earth energy up into your breath from those same very roots that you've created previously and bring them up in a much quicker fashion. Not simply following a trail of chains or a trail of roots but filling up every square atom in your body. Every form of cellular level must be drenched with the construct of the Earth energy. Fill your entire body. Sit with that energy for some time.

Now, remember each time that you're breathing inward, you are breathing Source itself. Every time that you are breathing out, you are releasing resistance, you're releasing trauma, releasing all things that do not serve you to hold for the greatest form of either neutrality or the greatest form of love.

Now, remember each time that you're breathing inward, you are breathing Source itself. Every time that you are breathing out, you are releasing resistance, you're releasing trauma, releasing all things that do not serve you to hold for the greatest form of either neutrality or the greatest form of love.

Pending if you are heavily mental bodied or heavily emotional bodied. If you're mental bodied you will thrive for neutrality. If you are heavily emotionally centered, you will thrive for great feelings of love. Either way, each breath outward allows the releasing of that resistance until you're perfectly tuned to the state of your previous desire.

Now, after grounding, we start the technique that we wish to share in this day. Your self-hypnotization allows you to enter the places of the subconscious. Now, of course, trying to find your unconscious and subconscious areas should be extremely easy for the majority of you.

You focus on your brain as the center of your mental body. Humans perceive that and coincide the brain construct with the mind and thought processes so, of course, symbolization of that brain as an organ will be our visual point and allowance of our energy entrance into the mental body and thought process.

Once the energy has been perceived, you can go into the stem portion of your brain to access that which is your primal portions of consciousness. This is what most humans will perceive as the unconscious and subconscious arena of the mind. And although this portion of the brain actually only represents the base function of your physical body in order to stay within your living state and be able to survive in the most basic form. This is also where the embedded conscious layers of your unconscious and subconscious would exist through the symbology and the meditation at hand. So zoom into the area that is your brain stem.

Now, for those of you who do not understand where the brain stem is, it is quite literally the low-hanging portion in the back of your brain that connects your neck and spinal column to the brain as a signal receiver and a giver. This part of that energy would be exemplified and would be worthy to dive deeply into. Now, of course, you perceive this part of your brain. You do not have to separate that part from the rest. You only need to focus on that part and start extracting those portions of trauma that would come to you.

Now, of course, before entering this energy, your intention must be heard. After your neutralization, after your grounding, after your heart-centeredness occurs then, of course, placing that intention initially that you desire to work with the subconscious unconscious layers and extract and remove that which is resistance and that which is trauma.

And in that moment you are doing quite literally this. You will be extracting all of the forms of energy that are the darker forms of purple. In this way, indigo is not deeply dark enough to be considered a form of purple in which this will be subconscious and unconscious layers extracting deeply into the root of that portion of your brain all the things that are deeply condensed in color. You would perceive the brain itself as a very light purple. The energy that encompasses the violet chakra that is your crown and the indigo that is your third eye, but lighter towards that of the violet color. And extracting that which is much darker than that indigo which is part of the experiential process mixing. You will extract those deep and dark parts out of you.

In this moment, you may in fact remember a visual form of memory or an emotional response to the extraction of that energy, because you are quite literally allowing yourself to extract the energy out of the subconscious and bring it into your conscious awareness itself.

In this moment, you may in fact remember a visual form of memory or an emotional response to the extraction of that energy, because you are quite literally allowing yourself to extract the energy out of the subconscious and bring it into your conscious awareness itself. And in that process alone, it can be an extremely intensive form of energy, whether it is emotion, whether it is a form of memory, be warned that you must go through your emotional work in order to do all things when dealing with trauma.

Now, we understand as this is a preface for all other forms, meditations, and techniques that we will share with you. There are no techniques that we share that do not allow you to be at the driver's seat of healing. You must be at the driver's seat of healing for that healing to stay with yourself. If you are simply able to just heal yourself small portions at a time, of course, this is possible. But the greater growth cannot ensue until all of that energy is removed to the subconscious layers of yourself as well.

So, as you understand yourself to be the conductor of this train, the conductor of this symphony must continue forward. If it becomes so greatly overwhelming that you cannot push forward, then stop in that moment and revisit it after you have allowed yourself the processing.

If there's a visual memory, remind yourself that symbology works with the mind greatly. That often you will perceive something that symbolizes something else. This is for all of you who see some form of energy in your visualization that does not make sense.

You may see a fountain. You may see an animal. And you will say to yourself in that moment, those who are mentally forward and those who are more mental minded. Of course, you would say a fountain has nothing to do with sexuality in this moment, nor does an animal. I have not slept with an animal, nor have I had sexual relations in a fountain. But, the symbology of those energies is important. Those may incur hidden memories from your mind that way through visualization.

Yet, some of you may also bring memories that are not true. You may bring memories that represent or symbolize something different. So you must be open to that energy of understanding that all things that you will perceive may or may not be rooted in an actual point of history unless you desire to create that point of history.

Some of you have such great and large forms of sexual resistance it may be easier to envision some form of horrible atrocity such as a rape or a removal of your sovereignty than to go through all of the smaller ordeals in your experience. Yet, in that energy, it is important that you stay engaged with what you receive in that moment.

Now, of course, the processing form is to let go of these resistances. So, as they are coming to, mind yourself of the emotions that you're going through. Allow yourself to feel those emotions as you are going through them. Allow yourself to engage with those forms of symbols and memories as it were in that moment.

And if you need to focus upon that symbol, or visualization, or memory, or projection, follow where it takes you as your Higher Fractal Consciousness is always in assistance with you in moments such as this. It is taking you to the journey it desires for you to go into the least form of resistance in your releasing of resistance. And, of course, that is highly important.

Trust that the Higher Fractal Consciousness holds your greatest benefit to your desire.

Trust that the Higher Fractal Consciousness holds your greatest benefit to your desire. Those of you who fear the construct of those guides showing you something for their own benefit, you are not working with your guides in this moment. If you know your guides and have worked with your guides and they show into your own experience of visualization, ask them, of course, please stand back at this moment.

This is a personal endeavor that must be experienced with only the Higher Fractal Consciousness and myself and release them. And, of course, those that are guides to you, those that truly care for you and desire to help you will, of course, step away. Which will leave you to your moment of continued processing.

Some things will be so deeply, drastically different from what you perceived, you may perceive that this may take you multiple days to process. Multiple weeks to process.

What we suggest in moments as this in the same form of meditation, the same form of neutralization, instead of focusing upon your brain stem and extracting new forms, simply go to that same brain steam area, but pull out only the visualization and the energy of that symbol that you'd pulled previously. And place an intention that you are going to work simply with that symbol for the day. Nothing more.

Continue to go through this process, allowing yourself and the Higher Fractal Consciousness to consistently give and share the greater advice of the Higher Fractal Consciousness.

Allow the Higher Fractal Consciousness to share there's no entity that can tell you what your sexuality is.

In a moment where you feel shame for an act of sexuality that occurred when you did not take the sovereignty of another being. Where you did not create rape upon another. Where you did not harm another entity, but still hold shame from some form of belief. Allow the Higher Fractal Consciousness to share there's no entity that can tell you what your sexuality is.

There's no entity that can create shame for you. Only an allowance of yourself to feel in a negative place about yourself in that moment. You are not a bad person. You are not a slut. You are not some gigolo. You are truly a being who was exploring their sexuality in that moment.

And the reason why it feels bad is that this is the core essence of why you are extracting what comes from the subconscious, what is shared from the layers of subconscious that come to you through visualizations and through symbols. So that you are able to deal head on with the subject at hand.

Allow the healing essences to come into your expression and welcome them, whether they be hard or whether they be soft. Allow them. Allow the Higher Fractal Consciousness to share that advice at an exponentially higher rate than what you are allowing your own thoughts to run off upon.

If you feel the mental body start chasing where you are now, being the driver behind the seat mentally only and not allowing your emotional constructs, your energetic constructs, the Higher Fractal Consciousness constructs to follow pursuit, then start backing up back into the position previous to the mental body's escape from the meditation and technique. Continue this and, of course, we will share more techniques as we share different portions of this energy.

After working with this technique then the last technique that we show can utilize this to help you filter and heal a great deal of the processes.

Now we wish to share with you a bit more in clearing the energy that is behind the emotional and the mental bodies respectively. The energies that are related to your mental body have been covered.

The energy that is your emotional body is the same form of technique, the same preface with the construct of neutralization. The same construct with the intention set for yourself to clear the emotional body. And, of course, you can do these in succession of one another. You can express that I have already done my mental body clearing. Now I will move to that emotional body clearing.

Even if you are one who leads with thought, it is still vitally important to clear the emotional body as well.

Even if you are one who leads with thought, it is still vitally important to clear the emotional body as well. Even if you are emotionally centered or led human being, individual, you must still work with the mental body. Both of these are important. Equally important, regardless of what your disposition is.

Now, instead of visualizing your brain stem, you are going to start perceiving the heart chakra itself. And more specifically, start to zoom in and visualize your organ of the heart. Now, we wish for you to surface the energy in your own search internally for the organs as they are the best symbolic means of the energy that is lying behind them, beneath them, and in between them.

Think of the mental body and associate what physical portion of the body, most humans will express brain or head. If you do so with the emotional energy and, of course, the emotions are in every chakra, each chakra that exists within your body holds emotion. But, the embodiment of emotion, the symbol of emotion is always, of course, the heart.

Visualize the nature of the heart. Visualize the place in where all four ventricles connect with one another. The center chamber of your heart. The working force of the heart itself. This is where you visualize the very center portion.

And again, you start extracting the most dark form of green out of that energy. And, of course, your heart itself will be a very light green color. Somewhere that is between the color of grass and the color of pastel green. But you are extracting the most dark of the forest green, the near browns, and black greens. Extracting those from the center of the center chamber of your heart.

As you do so, the intention is to allow the symbols that come out of your heart, allow the perspectives, the visualizations, the actual experiences to help clear the emotional body itself, the subconscious of the heart itself, and allow that that is unknown to you and unseen to you to be processed, whether through direct memory or through symbology. Allow yourself in that same way that you dealt with the mental body to deal with this process. If it is overwhelming, visualize and not take all symbols as accurate. Only know that these symbols are there for a reason.

If you visualize something that is so drastically horrible to your perspective and it comes with a great realization that this is a true and suppressed memory, then what we suggest is stopping at that moment and address that energy in that clear moment.

Many humans hold great travesties within their own sexual form of energy from their perspective

that so deeply changed their own consciousness
that it is quite truly a hidden memory from
themselves.

Many humans hold great travesties within their own sexual form of energy from their perspective that so deeply changed their own consciousness that it is quite truly a hidden memory from themselves. And humans hide these memories from themself in order not to fracture their own consciousness.

Many humans perceive mental illness, such as that of bipolar, such as that of schizophrenics, such as this that are borderline and direct personality experiences. And those are called personality disorders and dissociations or borderline of this as well.

All of these diagnoses have the possibility of being simple fractalized consciousness. Majority of those are truly fractalized consciousnesses. When we say this, it does not appear to feel negative because we are always utilizing the terminology in which the verbiage expresses that all energies that are within consciousness are fractalized. But this is different. This is your lower fractal consciousness fractalizing more so than what it already is.

You already exist as a part that is a very conditioned layer. That is very much so a part of your compartmentalized human expression. But this breaks apart the compartmentalization and refractalizes it into very different forms.

This is how multiple personalities within those who can be schizophrenic and have multiple personality disorders, and have personalities built for each of these. It is so drastically strong to the human psyche that it can fractalize and break apart deeply those essences of your own consciousness that you perceive as yourself.

As you perceive that energy, allow yourself to heal. If a great realization occurs that you know can fractalize the consciousness - stop. Call upon those who you trust the most. If you do not have friends or family, call upon your guides to help you in that moment. There must be a level of support if you feel as if you are at some form of breaking point.

Now, of course, this expression is a very common occurrence for humans in their collective as the realizations of sexual trauma that occurred previous in their life start surfacing. Many entities who are molested and raped by those that are in their family, such as their fathers, mothers, or relatives, often are deeply buried within the psyche of most humans who go through that experience.

Most entities do not remember the rape or molestation of themselves by this loved person until they reach a great form of adulthood. Normally, throughout the processes of your early thirties and late forties. And that is due to the nature of how compartmentalization works.

The longer that a human exists in the Earth Collective Consciousness, with more separations occurring each moment that they exist, the compartmentalization becomes a centralized form of your consciousness.

The longer that a human exists in the Earth Collective Consciousness, with more separations occurring each moment that they exist, the compartmentalization becomes a centralized form of your consciousness. And once this occurs, the opportunity for subconscious hidden memory resurfacing becomes greater. The consciousness that can occur in that moment can create greater psychological feelings of separation and disconnection. This is why it is so vitally important for you to find a support system in that moment.

Now, of course, we understand the majority of humans do not work well with a construct of that which is psychologists, that which are psychiatrists. And we understand the Western forms of medicinal energy based towards the energy that is known as psychological health or mental health itself is not a system that has been secured by any means. Is not a system where they are teaching the essence of human psychology.

But there are many of those that are counselors, many of those that work within that layer of energy that are extremely helpful to other humans, even if they are not trained to understand the human psychology and the human psyche deeply enough. If they are truly desiring to help another human, this may be all that is required for you to heal and to work with.

If you have no other human and cannot feel as if you are reaching your guides, go to those that are responsible for simply listening to humans. Your help lines that are created within the internet, crisis hotlines, suicide hotlines, any form of an experience where another human may share their perspective with you or simply receive and listen to what you are sharing. It is of vital nature for that to occur in order to have the energy of overwhelm not become a fractionalization of your consciousness and break apart that which is your personality.

So in that way, when you perceive those energies, it is vitally important for you to recenter and to hold support. Now, of course, the energy itself is an entirely different aspect. You have already spoken of the mental body. We have already spoken of the emotional body. But the energy that occurs through sexual trauma is a drastically different animal, as you would say.

The consciousness itself is a part of a system of co-creation where another consciousness and other entity are intertwining their own energy fields with your own in acts of sexuality. This becomes more personal as you are taking on the energetics of another entity. Where in the moment, where your sexuality connects the chakras against one another in the second chakras and the energy is being expressed through the explosive means of orgasm being shot out or simply reverberated. The energy entanglement becomes large.

This is why a great deal of you who have been in long-term or short-term sexual relationships have expressed that you feel bound to this person.

This is why a great deal of you who have been in long-term or short-term sexual relationships have expressed that you feel bound to this person. Even though your psychology expresses that it is no longer a possible experience to continue or not viable in your experience, you still feel deeply tied to that person. Now, of course, part of this is psychological. Part of this is the social nature of animal in which you came from in your second density of being jumped farther ahead created more remnants of that animalistic form of consciousness to follow you. So, of course, that energy is part of this.

But, a great deal of that is ties of energies and consciousnesses with you and those that you have had trauma with. If you have not cleared that trauma their energy is also a part of yours. Their energy is still entangled upon some forms, or some way, or some place within your chakra system, within your energetic bodies, within your mental or emotional states of consciousness.

So in order to rid yourself of this the techniques that are important are a simple cleansing of the chakra areas. And, of course, there are millions of ways in which this can occur. Our own suggested route is doing so as you did with the root chakra in your neutralization but start from the crown area.

Bring in the white light source energy into the crown, allowing all of the color of the violet to trickle down through that energetic porting of your crown chakra into the third eye. Then allow white light to enter this and take both the violet and indigo colors that were from the previous chakra and this chakra and allow it to go down into the throat chakra region.

And, of course, do this again and continue until you have you have gone into your root chakra. And then allow yourself to disperse the energy in the same way that we have shared. Allowing it to go into the earth.

Then, when you are connecting back to the earth, all you are bringing in you is Mother Earth-formed energy. You are filling yourself with it as you would a neutralization. But you are also bringing in that same form from the bottom of your feet, from the earth, and also into the top of the crown from your grid system.

The chakra comes within the system of intake and output at two separate regions.

Now, of course, the visualization process is an important one. So it is important for you to know how chakra systems work. The chakra comes within the system of intake and output at two separate regions. One is directly from the earth below you, which goes up into your feet, and into your root chakra, and up into your heart. And at the same time from the electromagnetic grid system, the ley lines as most humans call them, come down from the electromagnotheric into your crown chakra and into your heart.

Now, at the moment of intake, they are not touching or interacting with any form of chakra. Even though it enters the root chakra and goes into the heart, it does not interact with the root, the sacral, or the solar plexus chakra. It only goes through them in order to enter the heart.

Once the heart is entered and the crown chakra goes through that of the crown, the third eye, and the throat, into the heart, then the ignition simultaneously occurs, expelling the form of energy from the heart chakra simultaneously, both upwards and downwards into each chakra.

Then interacting with them personally and collectively. Engaging the portions of energy embedded within and release back into the same areas in whence they came into the electromagnotheric grid above you and into the earth below you.

The visualization of this can occur in the same way after you've allowed from the crown chakra all of the way to the root, the white light pushing and releasing. When you start bringing back a green Earth energy, bring the white light into your crown at the same time. Allow it to fill your body of green and white light until there becomes a very beautiful color of mint. That is a mixture of pastel form of mint. And once your entire body holds that energy, then feel your release of that energy in the body.

This will not fully release all energies that are entangled with your body in one meditation. It will be a repetitive form each time, getting rid of more layers and remembering that if you're still allowing belief systems to give you resistance to your sexuality, you are gaining new forms of resistance and traumas as you are going by.

Be mindful of your belief systems as you are using the techniques and meditations in order to clear energy and prevent new forms of energy from coming in.

Be mindful of your belief systems as you are using the techniques and meditations in order to clear energy and prevent new forms of energy from coming in. Allow the consciousness of yourself to refocus on the energies in which you desire to create and to co-create. Allow yourself exponential forms of growth as it pertains to sexuality. And remember that the healthiest form of sexuality is one in which there are no inhibitions. One which only holds excitement and connection. And one that does not take away the free will of others.

Now there is one construct that we have not shared that we believe is of great importance. There is the construct of human relationships that are detailed into two formats. Let us express more than two, but two majoritively.

The first as all humans would understand this, is to have an open relationship. To have multiple sexual partners. Polysexual. Multisexual. And create a form of that which is able to go into any form of sexuality which you desire. Engaging with multiple partners. Even holding a relationship with one specific entity. But allowing both parties the free rein of sexuality to the whim, sexuality to the desire, and the sexuality to fulfill the form of heart.

Where in others they are completely working with only one entity. And this is a monogamous relationship. There are two entities that hold such great forms of love for one another, that they believe the sexual energy that they are sharing with one another is so sacred that only engaging with one another is appropriate use of that energy.

Now we understand those of you who are within a non-monogamous form of relationship may see this as a form of mind control. A form of control of systems or a form of religious control.

Yet those that are in monogamous relationships may see poly-sexuality or poly-relationship formatting to be letting your spiritual essence go to any stranger or any human without sovereignty of that experience of holding to true or deep love. But, of course, these are simply two perspectives. None of these are incorrect. None of these are correct. They're only the essence of your choice and desire.

We have expressed through the previous engagements about the energy of those that hold multiple forms of relationships and those who hold monogamous ones. But the traumas that occur within both are important to explore as well.

Reminding yourself that in the construct of monogamy, in the relationship that forms of

sexual urges towards others, can create forms of guilt.

Reminding yourself that in the construct of monogamy, in the relationship that forms of sexual urges towards others, can create forms of guilt. Even if your partner is expressing that they understand the sexual nature of a human being is to feel sexuality towards other entities and not to feel guilty. There can still be portions of guilt associated. There can be fighting between those two if neither of them or one of them does not feel good about themselves and feels insecure.

Then they will project onto the other person their own insecurities or a construct of cheating, which is the breaking of that agreement and having sex outside of your relationship. Now, of course, even this can be projected. One entity who sexualizes other entities outside of the contract and blames the other for doing so. Now, of course, there are multiple ways that this can occur, but these are some of the greater forms.

There are those who are in non-monogamous or open relationships. These entities hold resistance in the form of holding partners long term. The construct of sexuality often creates forms of jealousy in humans.

Even those who are highly evolved to not feel jealousy can be held within the fear that they may lose this one person that they hold dear to them.

Even those who are highly evolved to not feel jealousy can be held within the fear that they may lose this one person that they hold dear to them. Especially in those who are opening a relationship when they have been used to this one person or one entity for a long period of time.

That energy in that moment can cause a fear that if your partner becomes intimate with another person and the sexuality is more fitting, more aligned with one another, or simply if the personality is more so aligned, then you will lose them to that person. You will lose the opportunity for you to be deeply engaged.

Now, whether humans understand this or not, there's a great truth that those who are most compatible with one another will receive the most attention from that person, the most time from that person, the most affection, and the most intimacy from that person.

Now, whether humans understand this or not, there's a great truth that those who are most compatible with one another will receive the most attention from that person, the most time from that person, the most affection, and the most intimacy from that person. But this does not mean that a feeling form of energy must occur if that fear comes to realization.

All of these energies that surround both the fears of monogamous and non-monogamous partners all come from a fear of one's self. Comes from a fear of being alone. Comes from a fear of not being able to connect with your own sexuality. So as important as all of the things that we have shared are, as important as the techniques are, know these simple truths in order to help you not gain new forms of resistance.

If you are not taking away that free will of another entity, sexuality holds no form of resistance naturally.

First, if you are not taking away that free will of another entity, sexuality holds no form of resistance naturally. Even that of the animalistic and chemical desire is not a resistance. It is only perceived as a resistance because it causes social problems for most humans.

If an entity feels that they must engage in sexuality and cannot find a partner to do so, then masturbation is seen to be too boring or not stimulating enough. And this, of course, can be remedied by simply understanding your body better. Understanding the way to please yourself from the sexual congress of masturbation by yourself. Trying new forms of masturbation within yourself.

But the allowance and desire for intimacy is something altogether different. You can have intimacy with other humans without sexuality. But you can also have sexuality without forms of intimacy. It is an important part to integrate both into those relationships, be it monogamous or free, and allow yourself the engagement of that energy in communication. If you do not hold a feeling of an adequacy of your self, then all things can be spoken of through sexuality with your partners.

The energy of sexuality itself, if not holding on to the pains and resistances and traumas from previous sexual engagements, you can clear yourself to have a new form of sexuality.

The energy of sexuality itself, if not holding on to the pains and resistances and traumas from previous sexual engagements, you can clear yourself to have a new form of sexuality. Be it in a monogamous or non-monogamous relationship, remind yourself that the most important part of your manifestation is yourself. If you are open to be with others, then open your heart to intimacy with others.

We wish to express to all of you that through the exploration of yourself and your sexuality, you will find a great deal more insight about yourself than many of those topics and that is because this portion of your own consciousness is hidden more so from than most other forms of communication. So explore and do not hold onto the feelings that come and go. Of resistance, shames and fears, inadequacies.

If you know yourself to truly be desiring sexual co-creation for the betterment of your Soul, then you can achieve this as well.

We wish to bid you all adieu not only for this moment, but for this conversation. And wish to express that as we are sharing with you, we are connecting with your energy as a collective.

We feel you growing from our reflections. And because all of us are one, we too are growing. We wish to bid you adieu as we congratulate you for your growth and we thank you for ours. Adieu.

G reetings to all. This is Aridif. That is A R I D I F and this
is it spelled. We understand that all of you have queries
for this day. But before diving into those queries there are the
two things that we wish to express. The first above and beyond
all things that are expressed in this day to know, feel, and to
perceive that you are loved in our perspective is of the utmost
importance. And secondly, it is our greatest excitement, and
within that same great excitement in which we co-create with
you not only in this moment, but through all moments of your
linear time perspective.

Before diving into these queries we wish to express that
throughout co-creation we have shared a great deal of energy
about human sexuality, galactic forms of sexuality, sexuality of
a personal, creative form, and a co-creative form. And in this
day, we will take the last of your queries to bring this subject
henceforth to the head, as you would express upon the human
collective terms.

But, yet, there is always a great deal of consciousness
behind the internal queries that will allow you to take what is
understood and create internal queries for you to work with

upon your own Higher Fractal Consciousness. Subjects that work with the human collective are never ending in both queries and possibilities to find that answer. So we will take your queries at your leisure.

Thank you very much, Aridif.

Yes, of course.

As we were discussing so much around sexuality, could you speak to us about why and when sexuality was created? Does it reflect a larger dynamic or foundational energy of creation itself? And what is its purpose?

Yes, of course. Now, pending upon the construct of sexuality in which you are speaking will depend upon the origin and time of creation. If you desire to understand the simple construct of sexuality as a means in which consciousnesses come together and create a different form of life, this is started at the very beginning of the Universal Collective Consciousness. Once the atomic structures that you understood split apart, created new ways to form within their selves and through mitosis states create new forms of molecules and molecular structures. After the atomic structure settled inward.

And if you are going past that construct and looking into the second-density life, this was very soon after the Universal Collective Consciousness was created. Now, of course, humans perceive the Big Bang construct as the birth of your entire form of reality. Yet, the consciousness behind the creation of the universe was first in a state of desire to create and to fractalize, and fractalization was the precursor of all sexuality and for creation of new experiences and existence.

To think that a multiple consciousness, dividing itself into smaller consciousnesses, dividing itself yet again and again. This construct brought forward the archetype and blueprint in which sexuality can be created.

And after that initial form of settling, planets, galaxies, solar systems being created, then, of course, came second-density life soon after. Within less than 1.4 million years after. And of course, third-density life found its way within only a few million years afterward.

As all of you perceive the construct of twelve billion years to six billion years of lifespan for the universe. It is much older than this in the construct of which you understand. And of course, the universal construct is only created by consciousness that desires to experience a specific form of universe.

At the forming of the universe and fractalization archetypes of consciousness agreed the way that physicality would work, agreed upon the constructs and rules and regulations for the physics of that universe. Agreed upon the structure of fractalization in the universe. Understood that there would be large clusters of galaxies and those would be broken into individual, and those broken into solar systems with planetary bodies and satellites around them, and different structures within each form of planet initializing a form of uniqueness upon each. Each fractalization being different.

Look to your technology now and see that there are no two galaxies that are identical. You can look at your technology in your own solar system and see planets are extremely different from one to the other. And you could look inside your technology and perceive the solar systems also having a greatly different blueprint per.

So imagine the life forms fractalized below. Now the means of sexuality in which you understanded from a human sexuality. This was created not long after the first forms of third-density life in the universe took hold, completed its cycle, and by the third iteration from our perspectives and from our perceiving the lineage of energy behind humanoid consciousness and bipedal humanoid forms of consciousness.

This is where the first form of internal and external organs that were created for a specific purpose of sexual co-creation for the specific purpose of being a means, which was more complex, yet meant more sense for the obligation to co-create a planet in that experience and became the first humanoid archetype for sexuality. And of course, throughout that iteration, a great deal changed from all forms of humanoid bipedal consciousness.

And now the purpose for that energy is not simply for the creating of life, although it was the original form of purpose. But for the expression of what it is to go through second-density chakra and go through the fourth-density heart chakra as well. The journeys and themes preplanned, gave that archetype a means and tool in which to work through.

Hence the sexuality being not simply the masculine versus feminine, not simply the energy of sexuality or animalistic drive. Not only the love that is held deep in the heart, but an expression of action, an expression of creativity, and the drive within as well.

Thank you so very much for your answer to that.

Yes, of course.

One of the course members asked this question. They said it feels as if the healing that is occurring through this work involves more than this current incarnation. Does releasing resistance and sexual trauma through the techniques that you have shared also bring healing to other versions of us? Also, does this bring healing to our ancestral line? And can you discuss the mechanics of how this occurs?

Yes, of course. First of all, as you are perceiving the healing that you are doing in your own sexuality. Of course, it is not simply your sexuality that you are healing. Now, of course, pending upon your perspective, it will be different in how you perceive the greater healing occurring. But if you are that of a Type Two entity, you will perceive that your sexual healing affects that of those that are around you proximity-wise and energetically.

Also you will perceive that the energy in consciousness of the person and any lifetimes in which they are directly related and connected, that are not that specific lifetime, of course, would be a part of that experience and the healing process. And of course, epigenetically you are taking trauma away from that collective form of human energy that is passed down onto the child that is your own spawn or proxy.

And of course, if you are type one then the most fundamental truth reigns within your heart, mind, and Soul. That when one being releases a form of resistance, the entire collective releases a form of resistance. And the same that is said with those who add resistances upon themselves, the entire collective becomes slightly more resistant in that way. We do perceive that all of us are one.

This is why as we share this energy with your consciousness and you utilize the understanding, integrate the constructs, work on that energy, then your own consciousness heals the entire Universal Collective Consciousness and beyond through that auspice of creative, co-creative, and co-creative collective forms of healing as well.

Thank you very much, Aridif.

Yes, of course.

The next question is, a lot of humans carry guilt around sexuality on account of what they have been taught through religion. Can you discuss when, how, and why these religious teachings about sexuality came about? And specifically, what was the purpose of creating certain tenets for gender roles, sexual expression, and relationships?

Yes, of course. First of all, within the construct of your original premises behind that which created your religious ideologies, we cannot speak for the intention of the first person who thought, perceived, or expressed, but we can speak to the intentions of the collective forms as it moves forward. As you look at the entire collective consciousness, the energy that is religious orientation toward sexuality can be derived by multiple reasons, ideologies, points of interest, etc.

One of your major constructs was the ideologies of creating forms of shame through sexuality. And by doing so it created inhibitions in persons to create sexuality. Some of this came at times where there were too many entities upon a certain area, district, or region and could not support with the natural forms of resources in which they were.

Some came to those masculine beings who enjoyed their sexuality so greatly they would not go off to fight in wars with other entities. So of course, creating inhibitions upon that would create a form of slowing down or stopping certain aspects of sexuality. Creation for the shame of the feminine energy for sexuality came so that there was not a great explosion of population for that same reason as the masculine energy.

And of course, there are multiple iterations that deal with the central formats of consciousness around the religions themselves. Even that of Catholicism created rules and regulations towards that of the clergyman not to be able to reproduce because it would not allow them to come back to the church and claim their father's inheritance once the preacher had died and take the church's riches. So, it is based within either energies to control or energies to prevent certain expression of human reality within. And this is upon the human collective side of that energy in co-creation.

Yet upon sexuality that was taught through aspects of consciousness relating to extra-dimensional entities such as those that were the Annunaki, certain sexuality was taught to them to create better sexuality co-creation with that human. Very selfish purpose for them to create only for the pleasure of their selves. And in other races created forms of resistant rules and regulations around sexuality as to prevent the consciousness of the human expanding into the higher levels so that they were easier to manipulate.

Now some of those that, in your perspective, may be perceived as better intended entities, would teach humans of their own sexuality and try to work philosophies that were already predesigned and preformed in the human collective.

Yet this energy would also be utilized and dogmatized by those that were religious figures in order for them to create a form of that energy. So, of course, as the religious constructs prevented many humans from exploring their sexuality in a very healthy way, it only added to that greater collective forms of resistance and thus created ripples for the future. And with that energy implemented deeply and strongly after several dozens of generations, then of course, that energy in the collective was a standard form of control for the same religious ideologies to utilize against human factions for the purpose that they desired as well.

Thank you very much for your perspective on that, Aridif.

Yes, of course.

We haven't really discussed pornography in this course so far. I'm wondering if you could discuss the consciousness and intentions behind pornography? And can you also share how pornography affects the relationship that humans who are exposed to it have with their sexuality?

Yes, of course. Again, for the first entity who created a video camcorder or a camera that was creating the pictures that intention for the individual cannot be expressed. But, of course, for the collective what we perceive is that sexuality being such a taboo and being so persistently resisted in humans and suppressed. Then, of course, the utilization of that which is hypersexual will create a tension which thus turns into a monetization form for those who create the expression.

Now, of course, this will pend greatly upon the archetype of human in which you are, the energy behind the intention of the person in which you are, but this can do a great deal for the human collective and for the person and relationship or ships that they are in. And in that co-creational construct many entities utilize pornography as their own sexuality feels suppressed or the relationship in which they are co-creating with holds lower sexuality in which they desire.

So, the utilization of that pornography will be created to create hyperfocus upon sexuality while they are either trying to balance their own energy outward or whether they are utilizing it as a crutch in order to hold up the feeling of that suppressed forms of energy. Now, of course, the implications of this alone can be drastically different.

Some entities only think about sexuality more and become more frustrated within their sexuality. Others utilize it as a form of somewhat healthy release, as what they desire to do they cannot and therefore extended form of fantasization. And, of course, without an expectation and without further damaging the path of their own sexuality, it can be utilized as that form of release.

But, for the majority of humans, it can create a form, especially in that of your pornography of recent years, can create a focus upon over-sexualizing masculine or feminine being. Now, of course, we perceive that feminine entities are more so and more drastically sexualized and objectified within the construct. But within the homosexual forms of pornography, it tends to be an equal form of sexualization of masculine entities.

So of course, this creates a form of empty vessel in which you are able to release your sexuality upon the masculine form. It creates either a masculine entity or a feminine entity that can simply be the receptacle of your sexuality, with no emotional forms of attachment. Which disassociates those who already have great forms of resistance. And this creates a form of apathy in their sexuality and can create a form of sociopathy within their sexuality. Their sexuality becomes nothing but a human tool to release your own orgasm upon.

Now, of course, the opposite forms of sexuality can be forms of healthy if that energy of animalistic sexuality is desired between both partners. Where the love attributes are healthy, both parties enjoy utilizing that energy, or perhaps one partner even desiring for the other to perceive it because they do not care for it, but wish for that partner to become overly hypersexualized for the encounter that is in front of them. Even though there are less forms of this now.

That energy could be utilized with pornography if more entities utilize the heart chakra within their own sexuality. And as we have experienced previously, we do not mean utilizing the heart chakra in order to simply love another person and wish to marry them in great long-term forms of relationship. Of course, this can be the utilization.

But often the simple appreciation for the human that you are co-creating your sexuality with would be a creator that opens that heart space with that of animalistic forms of sexuality. And of course, in great pornography forms for those who participate in the creation of all of those sexual forms of resistance, both societal, personal, co-creative, and within their own sexual partners, can be drastically altered.

There are some humans who hold a form of sexuality that are very stable within their self. Their heart is connected and when they go to films, what they perceive is that they are creating healing for others through their own imbalances of sexuality. And within the intention of the actor or actress within that pornography, it can create rippling healing effects for those who are in the same form of center.

But those who utilize as only a need for the finances, as only participating for the benefit of financial energy and feel imbalance within their selves, of course, that imbalance ripples through those that participate in the watching of that energy. So, within the greater pornography idea, it is as all aspects of sexuality that we have shared, spoken of, and co-created with you. It can either have great forms of healing, great forms of resistance and all things that are between.

Thank you very much, Aridif.

Yes, of course.

Changing gears a little bit. You mentioned when you talked about the fractalization that led to some of the mental illnesses over certain events. But you also talked about the process where you said that certain events or experiences are sent to the subconscious, as the mental body is not equipped to fully co-create or deal with those experiences at that time. Is the subconscious unique to humans? Is it necessary and what is it truly capable of processing versus simply storing experiences that turn into beliefs? And if the subconscious is necessary, what is the most empowered, informed way that humans can work with it?

Yes. First of all, the subconscious is not simply or only a human tool of utilization. This part and form exists in all sentient entities that are within their third density or later progress of this Soul journey. But in humans it tends to be more front of the way of their energy in processing the\an that of most races.

Now what the subconscious directly is, is different for each race and utilized differently. But, for the human collective, the subconscious is the place in where experiences are filtered. Physical reality itself becomes filtered.

The experiences of all of your senses become filtered and the emotions become filtered. And it brings all of that energy in that cannot either be taken by the mental body or the emotional body, which in some form of human cases can be up to eighty percent of their entire experience and is processed within internally.

It is directly connected to your third chakra, first chakra, and second chakra, and in that order of importance and utilization. The third chakra holds as a part of the subconscious deeply, as it is your sense of self. And the energy that becomes filtered comes to the surface when you are in a moment of either great disconnection or great exception. And in the moments of disconnection, what is filtered through that subconscious process ends within the line of connecting the dots of other things previously processed, but not understood, or things that were understood and processed but not seen by that individual.

And the energy that connects within the conscious construct of that self holds the construct of allowing that process to go uninterrupted for lack of better terms. Uninterrupted and uninfringed upon are your processing the internal and external variety of experience that are similar to those that you have previously processed and will help draw the correct form of responsivity, the correct form of emotion, the correct energy of thought, and brings that to the forefront more quickly.

We spoke previously of the superhighway of consciousness that exists in the human mind. This is for that subprocessing unit to superhighway. So, if you're working with energy that is similar to another, it will bring that energy from that without fault, without emotion, and bring it to your experience.

We will give you an example. If you are working in a relationship with a sibling and you are having an argument about a certain subject, and that subject has never been perceived by either of you, then your subconscious may bring an argument that was similar in nature but off-topic with another person that was close to in your life. And the way after finalizing your process that was easiest for you to feel was anger. But the most and least resistant part of that experience may have been forgiveness and moving forward.

So, what it will do is first bring anger to you and then allow the processing of going past and forgiving more easily. So, in that way, it is simply a super-processor that cannot be worked with the mental or emotional bodies if the stimulation becomes too great. And yes, humans can work in that way with the subconscious at a great deal of terms.

But the most simple form of access in that energy is when in meditation. Where you are focusing on grounding your body, releasing your forms of whatever non-neutral energy, then start pulling Earth energy directly into your third chakra. Then into your first, then into your second, and simply express the intention to allow whatever has been processed to come as quickly as possible. And allow that energy to come to you.

There's another way that you can work more directly with the subconscious through the Higher Fractal Consciousness, but this will rely upon a great tuning for your own psychic networking and the ability to at least have a form of back and forth with the Higher Fractal Consciousness minimally where you are able to receive a signal at the movement after asking a query to the Higher Fractal Consciousness.

The way this would appear is simply placing the intention to work with the Higher Fractal Consciousness, asking your query, and allowing yourself to feel a response, a certain sensation, a certain emotion, or a certain thought that lets you know yes or no with the certain answers. And allow that Higher Fractal Consciousness to work with the subconscious so that the filtering process becomes more clear to you.

In both cases working with the subconscious will not always give you the greatest outcome that you desire. It will give you one of the easier outcomes to work with for that movement and eventually, after processing what is needed, then of course you find the answer both in the conscious, emotional, and subconscious layers.

Thank you so much, Aridif.

Yes, of course.

I have a question. I'm actually going to ask this a little bit out of order. This was near the bottom of the question list, but I think this probably goes as a nice follow-up to the question that was just asked.

You mentioned some natural processes that we could tap into and utilize that don't require our mental body or that are beyond the capabilities of our mental body. I'm wondering – and you just mentioned working with the Higher Fractal Consciousness – can you discuss some of the systems that are available to us that are beyond our mental body or unknown to us on the conscious level that we can activate and engage with through intention? That would be empowering and helpful for us?

Yes, of course. First of all, as we mentioned in the context of which we are sharing in that expressed context that you've received. What we were sharing at that moment, is the processing in subconscious works as that layer as well and the subconscious is a tool that is utilized without the mental body, but is done so underneath the surface for lack of better terms. So in that system we have already shared that way to work.

Now, with the Higher Fractal Consciousness the number of capacities to work with yourself are unlimited in the way that your imagination and your consciousness can shape your desire to work. The Higher Fractal Consciousness works with all layers internally to the body and works with all of that higher dimensional forms of energy. So it is already a part that is everything that you are. That is why we have frequently and always suggested the constructs internally to work with the Higher Fractal Consciousness on most things that the mental body and the emotional bodies cannot process.

When you are working in any layer it comes directly as a connection process from your internal consciousness to the Higher Fractal Consciousness and back into your internal consciousness. For lack of better terms, the Higher Fractal

Consciousness is the tool that is not within your mental or emotional body.

Now, of course, the way that you can apply this energy is endless pending upon your intention. As you are aware, meditation is a utilization for the human collective to work in their natural forms of energy without the utilization of that mental or emotional body. It needs to be activated fully in order to process that energy, which should be native and natural to all humans. But the energy that is in the natural state of your own consciousness is that same form of energy that connects to all processes and connects directly into the Higher Fractal Consciousness.

So of course, layering human that is occurring upon any given moment must be set aside. Imagination in how to visualize this can be within all of you. Some of you will choose to utilize part of an energy that sits directly within the center of your third chakra, and you will say to yourself, this is the area where all non-mental and all non-emotional energy lays. And this is where I will do this and where I will connect with that energy in order to spring forward the process that allows the energy to be implemented and processed external to the thought and emotion.

Some of you may utilize the chakra that sits between the heart and third chakra to do so. Others may need a more complex form of meditation and visualization in order to create a process that is similar.

We have worked with a human who had utilized their consciousness sitting in an office that was a factory high in the chairs above the entire building and would look outward and had a control panel within their front and levers and buttons beside them. Each of them had individual purpose to access things that the mental and emotional body could not receive. And once buttons were hitten, levers were pulled, would bring energy from these tools into the unconscious and directly to the conscious layers.

It is as complex or as simple as you desire for this energy to be created. But the process that works outside of your mental and emotional body all comes through the process of the higher fractal conscious connection. So if you work with the Higher Fractal Consciousness in the least resistant form, this can be the process that bypasses all other processes.

Now, of course, the only alternative to that construct that will work one hundred percent of your time is that if you let go of all human resistance. Now this in our own perspective for all the humans that we have co-created with, is nearly impossible, not only statistically, but in the levels of evolution at which you are cannot be achieved by the majority of humans that have ever existed upon the Earth Collective up until this moment. And of course, may be expressed and experienced as you enter later terms of your fifth and sixth density included as well.

Beautiful. Thank you so much, Aridif.

Yes, of course.

You discussed how important being present and being the conductor of the train is in this healing of sexual trauma. Is this true for all healing or is there some healing that occurs without our conscious intention? And how does this actually work? For example, when one is receiving energy work or healing from another being, person, or entity?

Yes, of course. Now, the energies that you are speaking of in other consciousnesses, other humans' modalities of healing, entities that are guides that work with you, of course, you can receive forms of healing in that way. But as we have expressed previously, when you are working outside of yourself they are always but a temporary fix to a larger form of problem.

The problem with working in the co-creation as such is that these entities did not create that forms of resistance internally with you. They did not create a form of mental and emotional walls that are placed around chakras, placed around parts and portions of the personality that were framed around your psychology. So, of course, they are able to help lift the resistance for that movement.

But what happens after they have done their job and they have stepped away from you and your resistance and thinking and emotions are still there? You are only going to recreate that resistance and pending on how well the modality works and how clear the entity's intentions and your ability to receive that energy works. And of course, this can be for one hour or it can be for one year, but regardless, that energy will continue to build itself upon.

Now, we are not saying that it is impossible to work with these energy's less conscious layer. But what we are saying is you must have some form of awareness of the healing that occurs for the healing to stay in a most permanent way.

For example, if you are afraid of heights, you do not simply one day magically get over the fear of heights unless you are confronted with either a subject that is at adjacent to that fear or the fear itself. Now, of course, there can be ways where you feel better about it, and after several times of going around, then you can break that fear. But it always takes a form of co-creation and internal self-creation for the finalization of that process.

So, in that way the conductor of the train construct is correct. But the conductors can work with autopilot. And the way that you work with a more autopiloted facet is start working upon energies behind the backgrounds of those resistances. So, for example, if you are one who holds resistance in your heart chakra, who has built several walls around that heart energy. The first construct would be that it is hard to connect with others through sexuality. That is your primary focus. But the energy behind the primary focus can be worked upon in other ways.

Finding experiences that are exciting with other people has nothing to do with your own sexuality yet helps the form of sexuality. So, in that way, if you are diving more deeply into the construct internally, that is the surface point and origin for that resistance and for that feeling of problematic energy responsivity. Then you are able to work on that in a less conscious effort.

Thank you very much, Aridif.

Yes, of course.

Can you discuss the effect, if any, having children has on sexuality? And I do realize that is a broad question. Especially in terms of people who had sexual abuse in their past.

Yes, of course. First of all, as you are working with a construct of children, this will pend mostly upon the entities in which work with these. Now, some of these expressions are to do with a singular person and the feminine entity who has birthed a child and the sexuality involved with that person. Others will be the query of how it affects a group or couple that has created children together.

Now, of course, stimulation of sexuality comes from most entities in the Earth Collective with either lacks of stress or severe stress pending upon your sexual responsivity. Pending upon that resistance within your sexuality and pending upon the personality archetype of energy.

So, of course, those experiences with your children that are blissful may take away the form of sexuality for those who are more sexually stimulated during more stressful and argumentative forms of events, and the other way, in vice versa, is true and in accordance with that human archetype who only desires to create calm environments and have problems within their own co-creation of children tending to be that which is opposite of calm, which is chaotic at its core. So, of course, the energy for that person may have their sexuality forms felt to be pulled away or removed.

Now, of course, there are many humans who are unaffected by the experience directly with children. But what we can share most entities who have gone through the process of holding a child internally and birthing a child creates a new full of sexuality for that human being.

Once the chakra system of another human are overlaid with yours, the characteristics of that entity may implement into your own consciousnesses. And by having two forms of chakras laid over one another in the second chakra region can enhance the greater form. Now, this does not mean that a female entity will create higher feelings of sexuality.

What it means is it gives them the greater opportunity to have greater forms of experiencing sexuality, even though the utilization of this often is counterbalanced with the experience of operating in systems that are distracted by the energy of not feeling sexual or by creating a form of needing to give nurturing love to the children and this becoming more important than sexuality.

So, the energy that is around the construct itself is much different in its responsivity, its experience, and the way that it works with all humans. But for those who couldn't find a comfort in letting go of their resistance and have had children can explore a slightly deeper - approximately twenty to thirty percent deeper - well of sexuality from what they were able to experience before. But it is only the circumstances that create the psychology, that creates the emotions, that create an openness for that energy as well.

Now, those who have had sexual trauma are already feeling forms of resistance. Now in having a child after directly having a sexual form of assault or a sexual form of energy is quite traumatic for both the entity that is feminine holding the child as a mother and the child itself.

Those who have created a form of co-creation with a child and feel the bond, but that child is the child of a rape that occurred or an incest that occurs can create a form of resistance not only in their own sexuality, but in their own feelings towards that child as well. So, it is very many layers that are placed upon an individual must understand the archetype of their own consciousness and their own predisposal to resistance before that sexual assault or sexual resistances had occurred previously.

Thank you very much, Aridif.

Yes, of course.

The last question that we would like to present to you is you discussed the Egyptians who worked with reptilian sexual energy. And others who chose not to tap into that energy because from their perception it could be quite violent. Considering that humans carry reptilian DNA and what we inherited, for lack of a better term, from the Annunaki. Can you describe the characteristics of reptilian sexuality and the relationship humans have with this type of sexuality?

Yes, course. Now, first of all, understanding the archetype of reptilian sexuality is and of itself a spectrum, as all archetypes hold. But for the majority of entities that are born into direct and non-opposing archetype of that reptilian consciousness hold sexuality traits that tend to be more in the mental areas of sexuality and in the more animalistic style of sexuality as humans would perceive. These are the very physical and very exchanged thought process of sexuality form.

Many races that utilize sexuality that are in a body that holds reptilian archetype fully and not hybridized, will often maintain the form of violence within their sexuality, or utilizing sexuality as, for lack of better terms, a competition in that way. So, with that sexuality, it becomes very deeply ingrained within those entities and archetypes.

This is why many humans hold the form of their own multiple portions of reptilian DNA inside of your own consciousness. And this is why there are many entities who desire great forms of violence within their sexuality or desire animalistic and mental forms of sexuality in a sense.

They are leaning more deeply upon their own reptilian consciousness that is embedded within, unless it is for a reason of great, for lack of better terms, mental forms of resistance, psychological forms of resistance, and within their psychology having created different forms of emotional resistances. Some that are psychopathic and sociopathic in nature, they often lean upon that energy because it flows in the mental without access to that of the emotional.

Now, of course, this does not mean that Reptilians have no access, but a human in co-creation who holds psychopathy often holds the form that is closest to the reptilian energy. But cannot experience or exude to their own emotional construct.

Now, of course, there are many humans who have simply had a great deal of sexual traumas and those traumas create the lack of ability to feel emotion. And not all who feel no emotion in sexuality are psychopathic or sociopathic. But it tends to be to the higher degree that those who are socially psychopathic mimic that reptilian form of energy more so.

TReb Bor yit-NE's race, of course, is a hybridized form of race of reptilian, and they chose to give their sexuality away to quit creating genitals in which they are able to form sexuality and created laboratory forms of birth. And did so because there was a pain that was involved in reproduction.

There were large protrusions upon the penis of the masculine entity and the feminine being would receive pain from that exchange. Much as some of your animals upon Earth do. And because they desired to not integrate painful forms of sexuality, they took their own sexuality away from themselves as a collective form by removing that form of energy after generations.

Now, of course, the energy of many of those reptilian factions that you understand and know, such as those of the Earth Reptilians, their sexuality is that of the standard reptilian archetype. These are the entities that mostly co-created with Egyptian forms of consciousness. These are the entities who would create forms of sexual attraction by showing another that you are interested in sexual co-creation, creating dream states in where that person would be raped or when that person would be harmed or hurt. Masculine beings that would go after other masculine humans that were not homosexual and create dream states of them being raped by masculine reptilian beings.

To the reptilian consciousness, this does show a lack of empathy and a lack of sympathy for the human if they understand the consequence of the psychology that works for that human. But, there are some who simply do not understand human sexuality in that way and are just exuding their own sexuality to the human consciousness. Most within co-creation do understand once they've achieved a level of their own internal understanding and age.

But, making humans uncomfortable is very much so a goal of some forms of reptilians that are in the more malevolent spectrum of that of the Earth reptilian consciousness. So of course, this archetype itself was given great revere by those that were Egyptian.

Seeing the Annunaki holding certain reptilian characteristics and knowing that their energy was that of reptilian. Not expecting a pure form of Earth reptilian beings or some humans would come to call them the dinoids and not perceiving their own consciousness within the sexuality. And once it did occur after they called upon that form, regretted and changed their own energy towards the creation furthering that experience.

Thank you so much, Aridif.

Yes of course.

And thank you so much for this entire co-creation, for all of the information, much of which I think has been shared in a way that hasn't been shared before with humanity. And thank you for your care for us and the love that you have shown us and just all of the energy and support. And on behalf of everyone, myself and Rob and everyone who has been involved in this journey, in this course, we want to truly express our gratitude and our thanks and our love to you.

Yes, of course. And we wish to share with you before disconnecting in this day that as you are going through sexuality, as you are going through the traumas that you have perceived, as you are going through the experience of letting go of resistance, understanding the form that we have always shared is the most important form for the human co-creation of contact. To understand you are loved is vitally important.

It is difficult for humans to perceive the love that is within their grasp at all moments. It is difficult for humans to perceive themselves as being loved by a universe that can be at moments seemingly malevolent in nature. But knowing that the existence of the universe itself was created in the auspice and condition and actual forms of energy, love that creates the form of physical and nonphysical realities that we perceive as vitally important. Of course, we love you. Of course, TReb Bor yit-NE loves you. Of course, Rob and John love you. Of course, those energies are expressed vehemently, and of course, frequently.

But the energy of the universe is there when no other entities are around. Where you cannot feel the love from another. The universe is that of love. Utilize the love when you cannot find the energy.

As processing through your sexual energy mostly involves the integration of more feelings of love, not only from the universe to yourself, but from yourself to yourself as well. As we have expressed, as one entity grows we all grow together. We wish to congratulate all of you for the growth that you are having now and we wish to thank you for the growth that you have given to us in this co-creation as well. We will bid you all adieu this day and for this subject as well. Adieu.

Rob Gauthier is one of the most respected trance channelers in the world. For more than a decade, he has helped thousands of individuals receive clarity on their life path and mission. Rob primarily works with three main guides - Aridif, Treb Bor Yit-NE, and Metatron - but has channeled thousands of ET consciousnesses. Rob is also an in-demand speaker and teacher and has been featured in many documentaries, internet shows, interviews, and books for his unique channeling abilities.

Aridif is an Ancient Pleiadian from Deneb. His race originated in the Pleiades star system. He is a 6th Density (5th Dimension) being and resides in a spectrum of evolution of the Soul that is much higher than ours. He is a master teacher and has shared a great deal of knowledge about human evolution, densities, dimensions, consciousness, and the structure of the universe. Aridif has also worked extensively with Earth and humans throughout history to share enlightenment and cosmic knowledge.

Made in the USA
Coppell, TX
26 May 2024